THE TWO WITNESSES AND THE
KEY OF DAVID REVEALED

PROPHET WILLIE H. ELLIS

ARMAGEDDON RISING AT JADE HELM 15

The Messenger
Copyright © 2014

A Covert Graded, and Proven
Thesis paper submitted in partial fulfillment
of the requirements for the master's degree program at
Minnesota Graduate School of Theology

Copyright 2015
By: Prophet W. H. "Bill" Ellis
1136 Private Road 8037
Lincoln, Texas, 78948

Armageddon Rising At Jade Helm 15
Copyright © 2016 by Prophet Willie H. Ellis. All rights reserved.

No part of this publication may be reproduced, stored in a retrieval system or transmitted in any way by any means, electronic, mechanical, photocopy, recording or otherwise without the prior permission of the author except as provided by USA copyright law.

Cover and interior design by Jeffrey Doblados

Published in the United States of America
ISBN: 978-0-69297-031-7
1. Religion / Christian Theology / General
2. Religion / Christian Church / General
16.04.11

Acknowledgments

My profound thanks extend out to so many wonderful people who have contributed in many diverse ways to the success of this spiritual work. My first and foremost thanks to God. I am thankful that He found me worthy to carry His final message unto the nations. This book has been some twenty-four years in the making. During these times, my dear wife, Joyce, has been my faithful companion during our thirty-eight years of matrimony. This bouquet of roses is for you my love!

My sisters, Barbara and Velma, and my late niece Carol have all given so much in so many ways toward making my work a success. I thank God for them all.

To my daughters—Stephanie, Theresa, Betty, and Cynthia; they have all supported in many ways. My gratitude is multiplied to all of you. My granddaughters McKayla and McKenzie continue to be that inspiration that provide the fuel that powers my Soul Train.

There is my brother Moses, who has shared prophecies given to him by dreams and numbers. These prophecies manifested themselves, and they have brought forth fruit. Thanks to you, Moses.

My grandsons Devon and Timothy began to prophesy at the ages of six and seven years old on major things that became part of this book. I thank God for them, and may they be forever blessed for their contributions.

My grandson Zion, who is six, was baptized just as this book was being completed. He is the true apple of my eye.

My nephew Wallace has been an almost daily companion from the very outset of my spiritual work. God has anointed him to understand these hidden mysteries in a way that he has been a revolving inspiration to me. I am so grateful to him for is faithfulness.

I can never give all the credit that is rightfully due to my ninety-four-year-old mother, Sadalia Ellis. I am forever thankful and grateful to her and my late father, Moses Ellis, for the things that they taught and instilled within me and my nine siblings. They taught us to love and respect God and to love our neighbors as we love ourselves.

I have so many words of gratitude to my friend Pastor L. O. Lang and my daughter in the ministry Clarissa Garcia for their unwavering support over the years. They have both been a great source of inspiration unto me as I labored on this message.

I thank the angels that God sent before me in Moscow, Russia, as this journey was beginning.

Many thanks to all my former staff and writers for the *Moscow Business Journal* and all my former staff from Moscow's Open Radio. You have contributed in many ways to this great work.

Finally, it was the great folks at Tate Publishing whose professionalism brought all of this to reality. I am forever grateful to the project manager and my editor and all of their staff who made it happen. Much love, peace, and happiness to all of you. My deep appreciation extends to all.

Contents

Preface 6

Introduction 8

Chapter 1 14
    What Is the Key of David

Chapter 2 17
    The Key of David Is Revealed and Defined for the First Time Ever by Prophet Ellis

Chapter 3 23
    The Washington Monument Is Certified as the Seven Golden Candlesticks Plus One for the G8

Chapter 4 28
    The Purpose of the Key of David

Chapter 5 31
    Two Candlestick Keystones Certified as a Rod for Measuring and Identifying the Seven Golden Candlesticks

Chapter 6 35
    Certifying the Rod of God on Washington's Masonic Apron

Chapter 7 40
    Key of David Unwrap Twitter's Hashtag Heraldry and Twitter Closes Thousands of ISIS Accounts

Chapter 8 45
    The Code Name "Hashtag" Broken and Analyzed and Validated the Key of David

Chapter 9 47
    The Code Name Pound Sign Broken and Analyzed and Validated the Key of David

Chapter 10 49
    The Number and Tic-Tac-Toe Code Broken and Analyzed and Validated the Key of David

Chapter 11 53
    The Hashtag's Y2K Code Broken and Analyzed and Validated the Key of David

Chapter 12 58
    The Chevron: a Shoulder Piece and a Reliable Key for Identifying the Key of David

Chapter 13 63
    These Twelve Memorial Stones Are Now the Great Seal of the United States

Chapter 14 68
    Life Signified the Twelve Stones and Hashtag as Key to the Future

Chapter 15 71
    Cleopatra's Needle Certifies the Resurrection of King David as America's 44th President

Chapter 16 76
    Phi Beta Kappa Golden Key Represents the Key of David

Chapter 17 79
    The United States' Inherent Obligation to Build the Lord's Temple in America

Chapter 18 86
    Prophet Ellis Is Certified as a Prophet by a Historical Record

Chapter 19 93
    Confirming Cleopatra's Needles as ISIS Two Horns

Chapter 20 97
    The Statute of Liberty: Her Seven Spikes Opens a Golden Door[1]

Chapter 21 111
    Evaluation of Thesis: Minnesota Graduate School of Theology at South Texas Bible Institute*

---

1 *These chapters were not included with the original thesis.

Preface

My master's degree thesis paper was already completed when I learned consciously that Operation Jade Helm 15 military exercise was coming to Bastrop, Texas. I live about thirty miles east of Bastrop. My spiritual gift to understand and decipher dark sentences provided me a quick understanding that Jade Helm was the Pentagon's code for the keystone, which became the US Great Seal. The US Great Seal is the substance of the twelve memorial stones of Israel's exodus from Egyptian slavery into Canaan, the land of the promise.

I wrote my master's degree thesis covertly through a second party that the spiritual subject became unwittingly as proven by theological authorities. In my thesis, I opened the United States Great Seal and the national seals of its G7 leading industrialized partners with the key of David. The national seals of these seven nations are what the Bible refers to as the seven seals.

The opening of the seven seals reveals a multiplicity of diabolical secrets of the nations. This includes the god of this world who is called Satan, the Antichrist. He is also called the eastern star, a code name for the sun, and the Statue of Liberty. The eastern star is always positioned east of the crescent moon on Islamic flags. This five-pointed inverted eastern star is called a pentagram. It is used intellectually in the world over by academicians and scholars to depict witchcraft and Satan. This pentagram inspired the design of the Pentagon's headquarters. The Pentagon's response to this revelation is Operation Jade Helm.

Operation Jade Helm 15 has an authorized and an unauthorized mission. The unauthorized mission is influenced by military officials who are aligned with the red states that are labeled hostile. That mission is to carry out the Antichrist's orders to snatch, capture, and kill the messenger of God who has exposed him. That exposure and subsequent killing are chronicled in the nineteen verses of the eleventh chapter of the book of Revelation.

The death and resurrection of God's messenger, who are called His two witnesses, triggers the sound of the seventh angel and the seventh and last trumpet. The sound of the trumpet is a biblical metaphor used to signal the beginning of war. This war is biblically described as a war between God's armies, which have now come down from heaven, and the armies of all the kings of the world who joins together to fight against the Lord. That war is called Armageddon, and it is chronicled in the sixteenth and nineteenth chapters of Revelation.

My spiritual gift to read symbolism has enabled me to read and articulate the Jade Helm 15 logo. It depicts by symbolism a war between Jesus and the Antichrist. The Christian cross is depicted as a sword turned upside down so that it cannot be discerned as a Christian cross. It is a fulfillment of Isaiah 29:11–20 that describes the artifices of the Antichrist who hides those things pertaining to this sealed book by turning them upside down.

An *x* (ex) shaped as an arrow takes the cross out symbolically by attacking it from all four corners of the globe. This represents all the nations of the earth who are gathered against the Lord and his anointed. The slogan "Master the human domain" are words originating from him who was made a little higher than man. He seeks to lead them into a pit of no return. The Jade Helm 15 logo is the Pentagon's shorthand confirmation of those things written in my master thesis.

The official mission of the Pentagon's Operation Jade Helm 15 is to train for all the urban possibilities that results from the opening of the US Great Seal and the revelation of the Lord Jesus and his rival known as the Antichrist. This book contains the grade and completed evaluation form that has been completed by the professor for Minnesota Graduate School of Theology at South Texas Bible College. This master thesis was written covertly and was unwittingly and accurately graded to prove and validate the most significant event in the history of mankind.

Included in this book are the revelations of a multiplicity of the earth's most golden secrets. These golden secrets have been the Antichrist's source of power since he was cast out of heaven into the earth. A poem inscribed in the pedestal of the Statue of Liberty and titled "The New Colossus" boasts silently of those golden secrets. The Colossus of Rhodes was one of the original Seven Wonders of the Ancient World. It is a beast with ten horns positioned in the harbor at Rhodes to honor the sun god Helios. It is the same beast with ten horns described in the 13th chapter of Revelation and worshipped as the sun by those in the earth. Many people do not know our sun as an eastern star. The revelation of this mystery has angered many who secretly oppose Christianity. The Statue of Liberty is rightfully called the "New Colossus."

Chapters 20 and 21 are not submitted as part of my master thesis because they have not yet been revealed. These two chapters provide the mysteries of the Statue of Liberty and also the mysteries of God's two witnesses. Also included in chapter 21 is the first known photograph ever taken of an angel. God has sent forth His two witnesses in both a human form and an angelic form. It is a mystery that I shall make no attempt to fully explain. The Lord once said, "If you have not understood or believed earthly things, then how shall you believe and understand heavenly things."

The execution of the nine Christians in a South Carolina black church and the subsequent burning of seven other Southern black churches are all a part of the spiritual warfare for which Operation Jade Helm 15 is now preparing. It is a sign of Armageddon rising.

The poem that is inscribed into the pedestal of liberty ends with these words: "I lift my lamp beside the golden door." That door is now opened, and no man by any means can close it.

Introduction

This paper is the conclusion of an exhaustive and historic investigation to determine if the Key of David Project before the United States Congress is authentic. I have concluded by my investigation that this proposed legislation has merit. My investigation has concluded that the United States has a classified and an inherent obligation to build the Millennium Temple of God inside the United States under the leadership of the Freemasons. I shall prove these facts from the access that has been granted unto me by one of the most significant prophetic libraries ever to be assembled in postbiblical history. Among the things I shall prove and the historic questions that I shall answer are these:

What is the Key of David? Can Prophet W. H. "Bill" Ellis be certified as the promised messenger unto the nations? Has the Key of David ever been defined?

What is the purpose of the Key of David? What are the distinctive characteristics that makes it a key?

What is a keystone?

What is the Stone of Scone that King Edward I seized from the Scots in 1296, which became the coronation stone for the kings and queens of Great Britain?

Why is this stone also called the "Stone of Destiny"?

Is this great stone a key to something that has remained secret with the nations and the Scottish Rite Freemasons?

Is this the stone that Jesus called a white stone and the hidden manna in Revelation 2:17?

Are these the great stones that God hid, as mentioned in Jeremiah 43:7–10?

Is it the stone that Jacob put for his pillows at Bethel and set them up as a pillar?

Is this stone the white Egyptian pillar, which we call the Washington Memorial, and Dr. King called the Stone of Hope?

Are these the stones laid before Joshua, which Joshua said, "Shall be a witness unto Israel lest it deny its God"?

The Key of David has opened a golden door where all these answers can be found.

Yet my research has found and can defend the answers to many other related questions that will reveal and confirm the Key of David. Among these questions are, "What stone was Jesus speaking of in Matthew 21:42–46, when he asked the chief priests and Pharisees a simple question about a stone that the builders rejected? Why did they think he was talking about them when he said, "The Kingdom of God shall be taken from them, and whosoever shall fall on this stone shall be broken: but on whomsoever it shall fall, it will grind him to powder"?

Is this stone the same stone associated with the kingdom of God that was shown to Nebuchadnezzar in a frightening dream in Daniel 2:31–46 and which dream Daniel interpreted for the king, telling him that this is what shall come in the last days, when he shall have dominion over all men?

What are the mysteries of the two stone pillars that are called Cleopatra's Needles, which once stood before Pharaoh's house in Egypt? Why did the Freemasons move one of these two-hundred-ton candlestick-shaped pillars to the banks of London's River Thames in 1877, where it remains standing today? Why did they move its twin in 1880 to New York City Central Park, where it remains today? Is there a relationship between these two stone pillars called Cleopatra's Needles and the needlepoints of the Master Mason's emblem, which they call their cornerstone?

What stones were Satan speaking of in Matthew 4:3, when he said to our Lord, "If thou be the Son of God, command that these stones be made bread"? What inspired the nickname for the state of Pennsylvania whose nickname is called the "Keystone State"? Is the Phi Beta Kappa golden key and the formation of the fraternity on December 6, 1776, related to the US Declaration of Independence on July 4, 1776, in Philadelphia and the Key of David?

When God spoke to the high priest Joshua and the fellows who were with Joshua in Zechariah 3:9–10, God said he would bring forth His servant the branch with the stone laid before Joshua. The two candlesticks and two olive branches are what God called His two witnesses in Revelation 11:1–19. Is this the same stone that the other Joshua in Joshua 24:26–27 said shall be a witness unto Israel, lest it deny its God? Is this stone going to be a key, which identifies God's messenger unto the nations? Is this why this stone is called a keystone and its secrecy is protected by the Freemasons? Does this stone have anything to do with the seven golden candlesticks? Could the seven golden candlesticks be what the leading industrialized nations refer to as the G7?

Why was the Washington Monument crafted in the likeness of Cleopatra's Needle that was moved from Egypt to London and to New York City Central Park? Since Egyptian minted coins honoring Cleopatra as their resurrected sun goddess Isis whose crown has two horns between a sundial, are these two horns symbolic of these two candlesticks stone pillars? Are these the same two horns belonging to the beast in Revelation chapter 13? Could there be a reason for the media and the nations not mentioning and associating the Islamic terror group ISIS with Egypt's sun goddess Isis? Could the beheading of Christians by ISIS be the same end-time beheading of Christians chronicled in Revelation 20:4, saying, "And I saw thrones, and they sat upon them, and judgment was given unto them: and I saw the souls of them that were beheaded for the witness of Jesus, and for the word of God, and which had not worshipped the beast, neither his image, neither had received his mark upon their foreheads, or in their hands; and they lived and reigned with Christ a thousand years."

Are these thrones the same thrones where God hid these great stones with the king of Babylon mentioned in Jeremiah 43:7–10? And whose pavilion has now spread globally as spoken by God? Is this the reason that Babylon appears as a mystery in Revelation 17:4–11 whereby she is decked with these precious stones as a harlot? Consider the following scriptures:

> And the woman was arrayed in purple and scarlet colour, and decked with gold and precious stones and pearls, having a golden cup in her hand full of abominations and filthiness of her fornication: And upon her forehead was a name written, MYSTERY, BABYLON THE GREAT, The MOTHER OF HARLOTS And ABOMINATIONS OF THE EARTH. And I saw the woman drunken with the blood of the saints, and with the blood of the martyrs of Jesus: and when I saw her, I wondered with great admi-

> ration. And the angel said unto me, Wherefore didst thou marvel? I will tell thee the mystery of the woman, and of the beast that carrieth her, which hath the seven heads and ten horns.
>
> The beast that thou sawest was, and is not; and shall ascend out of the bottomless pit, and go into perdition: and they that dwell on the earth shall wonder, whose names were not written in the book of life from the foundation of the world, when they behold the beast that was, and is not, and yet is. And here is the mind which hath wisdom. The seven heads are seven mountains, on which the woman sitteth. And there are seven kings: five are fallen, and one is, and the other is not yet come; and when he cometh, he must continue a short space. And the beast that was, and is not, even he is the eighth, and is of the seven, and goeth into perdition. (Rev. 17:4–11)

I will show this is what is called the G7/G8 nations.

Is this the stone that God laid and His angels pick it up and toss the stone into the sea causing Babylon to fall never to rise again?

Jeremiah 43:7–10 chronicles where God hid this stone in Egypt at the entry to Pharaoh's house. Jesus mentioned that this stone shall become a millstone to whosoever should fall on it. The following scripture shows where the angel of the Lord moved both the stone and the candle from Babylon causing her to fall. I will defend and show that this fall was the fall of the second super power that came to be known as the Soviet Union.

> And after these things I saw another angel come down from heaven, having great power; and the earth was lightened with his glory. And he cried mightily with a strong voice, saying, Babylon the great is fallen, is fallen, and is become the habitation of devils, and the hold of every foul spirit, and a cage of every unclean and hateful bird. Rejoice over her, thou heaven, and ye holy apostles and prophets; for God hath avenged you on her. And a mighty angel took up a stone like a great millstone, and cast it into the sea, saying, Thus with violence shall that great city Babylon be thrown down, and shall be found no more at all. And the light of a candle shall shine no more at all in thee; and the voice of the bridegroom and of the bride shall be heard no more at all in thee: for thy merchants were the great men of the earth; for by thy sorceries were all nations deceived. (Rev. 18:1–2, 20–21, 23)

I will argue and clearly defend that Prophet W. H. "Bill" Ellis is God's messenger and two witnesses to the nations. He has provided and I have confirmed by research and investigation that Jesus has given him the Key of David. I shall defend my conclusion by providing clear, precise, and positive answers to all questions raised in my introduction herein.

My research and investigation has confirmed that this stone is the cornerstone and the key that signals the time to rebuild the house of God as shown to the prophet Ezekiel. The building of this house is an inherent obligation of the United States and its G7 partners for the favors shown to them by the Most High God. This inherent obligation is the substance of the Key of David project submitted to the full US Senate and house members. It is an obligation which the United States and its G7 partners no longer intends to honor, but it is also one that cannot be circumvented. A twenty-three-year prophetic record complied by Prophet Ellis during his spiritual guided search serves as an estoppel for those seeking to challenge his legitimacy as God's messenger. Such authority comes also with power which cannot be successfully ignored.

An unconscious, spiritual, systematic, and well-documented methodical twenty-year search for the Key of David began by Prophet Ellis on March 7, 1992, in Moscow, Russia. It has now culminated into what is undoubtedly the largest prophetic library in postbiblical history. This also includes what is essential to every legitimate prophet. That essential item is a dream diary whereby God's instructions are carefully recorded. Prophet Ellis's diary began on April 27, 1998, and has continued until this day. It is believed to be the largest systematic record of dreams ever by any person. It includes the subject, date, and time of each message that cannot be debunked by the opposition. I have been granted full access to it and his complete prophetic library for this master degree thesis. God spoke to Aaron and his sister Miriam, the brother and sister of Moses, and told them that He would speak to His prophets in dreams (Numbers 12:4–8). Therefore, such prophetic diary is essential.

Significantly, on Christmas Day 1991, the Soviet Union collapsed. Three months later on March 7, 1992, Prophet W. H. "Bill" Ellis would arrive in Moscow unaware that he was being led by the Spirit of God on a search for the Key of David. He would arrive as a western businessman who would be founder and publisher of the *Moscow Business Journal*. Within three months of his arrival, he would produce a five-day-a-week radio business program which he called "The Moscow Business Journal Report." It kept both Russian and western businessmen up-to-date on this newly established market economy as they sought to make their fortunes in this new transforming Russian Republic.

The ease, by which he rose rapidly through the business and government sectors there, caught the eyes of many including the White House. He appeared on various television programs who wanted to know how he was able to accomplish such so fast and so easy. He had no simple answer. He was unaware of his spiritual mission and the biblical mysteries that had been hidden behind what Winston Churchill called the Iron Curtain.

He became one of the founding honorary members of the *Moscow Times*, which today is Moscow's leading English language newspaper. Both *Voice of America* and *BBC* broadcasted from *Open Radio*, where he produced his daily business program. He managed to interview such nobles, Mikhail Gorbachev and Boris Yeltsin, for both his magazine and his radio program. He was tapped by the Clinton administration to take part in the historic "Partnership for Progress Summit" for the Newly Independent States (NIS) held at George Washington University.

In the spring of 1993, a former communist boss, as they were called, would point out some racist symbols that had been hidden on Marlboro cigarette packaging along with a microscopic Latin phrase, *veni, vidi, vici*.

This revelation secreted on Marlboro cigarettes, revealed by this communist boss, would not only be a cover story for the new magazine but also it would be a vital road map to the Key of David some twenty years later. Hidden under Masonic symbolism on the packaging were three inverted "K-like" symbols on both sides and the bottom of the packaging that are draped over a white triangular marble stone. The three K-like symbols, according to the former communist boss, are the trademark for the white supremacist group known as the Ku Klux Klan. The Philip Morris Tobacco representatives were unprepared and chose to remain silent rather than deny the revelations. They would cancel their side of the interview and quietly remove the microscopic Latin phrase *veni, vidi, vici* from their packaging. Its English translation means, "I came, I saw, I conquered."

A deep spiritual study into the printing methods of Masonry revealed that the three *K*'s are interchangeable with their numerical place values in the English alphabet system, thus making the three elevens a hidden way for writing 33 for the 33rd degree of Freemasonry. When draped over the white stone, which is the keystone representing the Key of David, it symbolizes a key held and protected under the secrecy of Freemasonry. This is the stone that Masonry calls their cornerstone. It is represented by their compass and square. It is the same white stone mentioned by Jesus in Revelation 2:17 and shown to and hidden with Nebuchadnezzar, the king of Babylon, a man whom God raised up as the founder of the Soviet Union.

During these revelations, Prophet Ellis was unaware that he was being led to the Key of David by the Spirit of God. Still there were much more to come and learn from Marlboro package design. It would be more than six years before it is revealed that the emblems belong to Freemasonry.

My research and investigation has confirmed that the Key of David could not have properly worked without the fall of the Soviet Union first. The key is two candlestick-shaped stone pillars that stood before Pharaoh's house during the days of Moses and Israel's exodus from Egyptian slavery. Each candlestick-shaped stone measures a precise 69.375 feet tall, which is the key benchmark for identifying the original seven golden candlesticks that were hidden in the US Capitol. These seven golden candlesticks are what the seven leading industrialized nations refer to themselves as when they call themselves G7. These two candlestick stone pillars are what God calls His two witnesses in Revelation 11:1–19.

Understanding the following mathematical illustration is paramount toward identifying the two candlestick stone pillars as a keystone. The twelve memorial stones of Israel that represents the twelve sons of Jacob have been joined together. Thus, they have gone from being a pillow to a pillar. This chronicles in Genesis 28:15–22 in Jacob's ritual at Bethel.

> And Jacob rose up early in the morning, and took the stone that he had put for his pillows, and set it up for a pillar, and poured oil upon the top of it. And he called the name of that place Bethel: but the name of that city was called Luz at the first. (Gen. 28:18–19)

This new name is essential to understanding this mystery. This is because it is the same stone which Jesus called the hidden manna with a new name written therein in Revelation 2:17. This pillar is the same pillar that is mentioned in his temple along with his new name and the New Jerusalem in Revelation 3:12.

> Him that overcometh will I make a pillar in the temple of my God, and he shall go no more out: and I will write upon him the name of my God, and the name of the city of my God, which is new Jerusalem, which cometh down out of heaven from my God: and I will write upon him my new name. (Rev. 3:12)

After Jacob's ritual at Bethel, he made a vow that ended with him declaring that this stone, which he set for a pillar, shall be God's house. Therefore, this pillar is confirmed as a candlestick by Jesus in Revelation 1:20 when he reveals the mystery of the seven stars and the seven golden candlesticks. He defined the seven candlesticks as the seven churches. Jacob proclaimed the pillar to be the house of God. Thus, it is settled that the stone is hereby verified both biblically and physically as being a pillar in candlestick form.

> The mystery of the seven stars which thou sawest in my right hand, and the seven golden candlesticks. The seven stars are the angels of the seven churches: and the seven candlesticks which thou sawest are the seven churches. (Rev. 1:20)

Jacob's words shall bear witness to this.

And Jacob vowed a vow, saying, If God will be with me, and will keep me in this way that I go, and will give me bread to eat, and raiment to put on, So that I come again to my father's house in peace; then shall the Lord be my God: And this stone, which I have set for a pillar, shall be God's house: and of all that thou shalt give me I will surely give the tenth unto thee. (Gen. 28:20–22)

These twelve stones went on to be the twelve memorial stones of the exodus that were lain in Jordan. They have now been joined together from a pillow to a pillar which stands exactly 555 feet tall, which we recognize in our nation's Capitol as the Washington Monument. It is the substance of seven golden candlesticks plus one for Russia—the G8.

Now by using simple arithmetic, I will identify and certify the two stone pillars in candlestick form as the actual keystone. Its precise height of 69.375 feet is a benchmark, pin number, and a key that unlocks a secret golden door to the seven golden candlesticks of Israel. It is the token for God's two witnesses. It is the symbolism for the two bars on the Israeli national flag on opposite sides of its Star of David.

The height of 69.375 feet times 7 is equal to 485.625 feet—this being the height of seven golden candlesticks for the G7 nations. After the fall of the Soviet Union, Russia joined the G7 and became the G8. Therefore, 69.375 additional feet is added to 485.625 for the total sum of 555 feet tall.

I will show that the answer to all questions raised in my introduction is "yes." I will show that after Prophet Ellis released the mysteries of this key in a widely circulated press release that his opponents quickly implemented a strategy to debunk it. His press release was dated January 20, 2015. Efforts to debunk it were released by major news organizations on February 17, 2015.

On February 17, 2015, the *Los Angeles Times* and other news organizations reported that the Washington Monument was now shorter than 555 feet. This announcement came after the Council on Tall Buildings and Urban Habitat decided upon a new starting point for its measurements. The monument now measures, according to their report, 554 feet 7 and 11/32 inches.

Chapter 1

What Is the Key of David

Since time, which cannot be measured, the Key of David has remained a hidden and undefined divine secret until now. Because of its powerful purpose and divine nature, no man could have defined or revealed it, but hc that has received it. The key is the substance of two great three-thousand-year old stone pillars that stood before Pharaoh's house during the days of Moses. Today, one stand on the banks of London's River Thames, and its twin stands in New York City Central Park at a precise height of 69.375 feet in candlestick form. They are the two candlesticks that God called His two witnesses in Revelation 11:1–19. They are also the same great stones mentioned in Joshua 24:26–27 that Joshua proclaimed shall be a witness unto Israel lest it deny its God.

The stones are a key evidencing God's power and authority given to the seven leading industrialized nations and the churches within these nations.

> Remember therefore from whence thou art fallen, and repent, and do the first works; or else I will come unto thee quickly, and will remove thy candlestick out of his place, except thou repent. (Rev. 2:5)

The precise dimension of the height of the two stone candlesticks acts as a key, which identifies the seven golden candlesticks hidden with the G7 nations, and it's the substance of the Washington Monument. The United States refers to this stone as the keystone, and it comprises the United States' Great Seal. This divine gift of favoritism inspired the nickname for the state of Pennsylvania, which is called the Keystone State. America declared its independence at Philadelphia, Pennsylvania, on July 4, 1776. Jesus proclaimed his Key of David to the angel at the church in Philadelphia.

The Key of David is divinely positioned to reveal itself as being genuine. It cannot be debunked by challenges raised by those who oppose God's choices for the ages. It is currently working and opening ancient and golden doors that are once locked. Simultaneously, it is shutting doors that once are opened. Once opened, no man can shut them, and once shut, no man can open them. These are the features of the Key of David, which Jesus mentioned in Revelation 3:7 in his message to the angel of the church at Philadelphia.

The revelation of the Key of David comes simultaneously with the establishment of God's kingdom in the earth. One of the purposes of the stone is to signal when His kingdom is being established. Since the Key of David is now revealed, so is the kingdom of GOD.

> And in the days of these kings shall the God of heaven set up a kingdom, which shall never be destroyed: and the kingdom shall not be left to other people, but it shall break in pieces and consume all these kingdoms, and it shall stand for ever. Forasmuch as thou sawest that the stone was cut out of the mountain without hands, and that it brake in pieces the iron, the brass, the clay, the silver, and the gold; the great God hath made known to the king what shall come to pass hereafter: and the dream is certain, and the interpretation thereof sure. Then the king Nebuchadnezzar fell upon his

face, and worshipped Daniel, and commanded that they should offer an oblation and sweet odours unto him. (Dan. 2:44–46)

As Daniel was interpreting the king's dream in Babylon, God was having the prophet Jeremiah hide these stones symbolically in Egypt where he and a remnant of Judah had fled after Judah had fallen to Babylon. God would have Jeremiah to hide them at the entry to Pharaoh's house.

> So they came into the land of Egypt: for they obeyed not the voice of the LORD: thus came they even to Tahpanhes. Then came the word of the LORD unto Jeremiah in Tahpanhes, saying, Take great stones in thine hand, and hide them in the clay in the brickkiln, which is at the entry of Pharaoh's house in Tahpanhes, in the sight of the men of Judah; And say unto them, Thus saith the LORD of hosts, the God of Israel; Behold, I will send and take Nebuchadrezzar the king of Babylon, my servant, and will set his throne upon these stones that I have hid; and he shall spread his royal pavilion over them. (Jer. 43:7–10)

Jesus also left many coded messages concerning these stones that are hidden in Egypt at the entry to Pharaoh's house. In one, he would refer to the stones as the hidden manna. Manna was the bread that God fed to His people during their forty-year exodus from Egyptian bondage. These were the same stones that Satan referred to when he sought to tempt Jesus after the Lord had fasted for forty days. Therefore, Jesus would send a message to the church in Pergamos that he knows where Satan's seat is when referencing the stones that God had hidden with Satan and all his kingdoms of the world.

> And to the angel of the church in Pergamos write; These things saith he which hath the sharp sword with two edges; I know thy works, and where thou dwellest, even where Satan's seat is: and thou holdest fast my name, and hast not denied my faith, even in those days wherein Antipas was my faithful martyr, who was slain among you, where Satan dwelleth. He that hath an ear, let him hear what the Spirit saith unto the churches; To him that overcometh will I give to eat of the hidden manna, and will give him a white stone, and in the stone a new name written, which no man knoweth saving he that receiveth it. (Rev. 2:12–13, 17)

Notes

- Related Titles: "Stone of Destiny," by Dr. Hugh Findley. Library call Number PS-3511 154 58, printed in the year of the great ice storm and big wind (1940). Dr. Findley was a prominent landscape Architect of New York. He was born in Ayr, Scotland where King Edward I sized this stone and brought it back to London. The Coronation Chair in Westminster Abbey was built to enclose this stone. The oath taken by the kings and queens cite that their throne is the future throne of David. This stone is therefore called a keystone representing the Key of David.

- Dr. Findley was brought to the United States in infancy by his parents. He studied at Clark University, Worchester; Cornell University, Syracuse University (B.S.A.), Columbia University, (M.A.) and at Harvard where he received the M.L.A. degree. He was a distinguished Professor at the University Of Texas School Of Architecture.

One of his many cunning poems alluding to this stone that was hidden by God carries the title "The Star Sapphire and The Rose". His poem, says: I wrapped my red rose in a prayer, and dreamed that you were hidden there, beneath it petals, quite alone, for in the sapphire's sky-blue stone. Its star cannot be far away when two can prey.

Note: what made this poem famous among the elite is the truth of its cunning words. The red rose was the House of Lancaster badge during the British "Wars of the Roses". This is where one of the stones is hidden on the banks of the Thames River.

Dr. Findley calls it a Sapphire stone because it is described as a sapphire stone in Ezekiel 10:1 where it appears as the throne of the man clothed in linen. Ezekiel 9th and 10th chapters is where Vladimir Lenin the Founder of the Soviet Union adopted his new name. Lenin was born Vladimir Ilyich Ulyanov on April 23, 1870. He changed his name to Lenin when he came to power during Russia's October Revolution of 1917. This sapphire stone is associated with his end-time throne in Ezekiel, saying,

"Then I looked, and, behold, in the firmament that was above the head of the cherubims there appeared over them as it were a sapphire stone, as the appearance of the likeness of a throne. And he spake unto the man clothed with linen, and said, Go in between the wheels, even under the cherub, and fill thine hand with coals of fire from between the cherubims, and scatter them over the city. And he went in in my sight" (Ezek. 10:1–2).

Other References: Charting The End Times (Tim LaHaye & Thomas Ice). Copyright (2001) Pre-Trib Research Center. Published by Harvest House Publishers. Dr. LaHaye's book uses charts to illustrate that the revelation of this stone signals the judgment of the nations, and the end of gentile power. It is considered as unlawful to write in any manner other than codes concerning this stone. Dr. LaHaye used only graphics.

Related sources: Messiah's Coming Temple by John W. Schmitt & J. Carl Laney: (1977) ISBN 0-8254-3727-x. Ezekiel's Vision of the Future Temple.

Chapter 2

The Key of David Is Revealed and Defined for the First Time Ever by Prophet Ellis

Many scholars and academicians have sought in vain to define the Key of David. This includes the Rev. Gerald Flurry whose Philadelphia Church of God produces the television show called the *Key of David* hosted by Flurry. Their inability to define it holds true to the words spoken by Jesus to the angel of the church at Pergamos. That is, no man knows about this stone but he who receives it.

This section gives the most coherent answers that I have pulled form gotquestions.org on what is the Key of David. Many have chosen not to make any attempt to answer a question whose answers God has kept sealed for His messianic messenger. The purpose of section two is to compare the most coherent answers available to those of Prophet Ellis's. A fair comparison would confirm his as being superior, authoritative, and correct. The two I've chosen from gotquestions.org shall follow.

Question: What is the Key of David?

Answer: The Key of David is a term found in Revelation and Isaiah. A key indicates control or authority; therefore, having the Key of David would give one control of David's domain, i.e., Jerusalem, the city of David, and the kingdom of Israel. The fact that in Revelation 3:7, Jesus holds this key shows that He is the fulfillment of the Davidic covenant, the ruler of the New Jerusalem, and the Lord of the kingdom of heaven.

However, the passage in Revelation has been used inappropriately by a number of cults that ultimately descend from the Christian Identity Movement via Armstrongism. The Philadelphia Church of God, a splinter group from the Worldwide Church of God, produces a television program called *Key of David*.

Scriptural usage: the Key of David is most directly referenced in Revelation 3:7, "To the angel of the church in Philadelphia write: these are the words of him who is holy and true, who holds the key of David." The Old Testament reference is Isaiah 22:22. There, the prophet tells the palace secretary Shebna that he will be replaced by Eliakim, for God "will place on his shoulder the key to the house of David" (Isa. 22:22). The one who holds the keys has the authority. Thus, the Key of David implies control of David's domain, which was promised to the Messiah in both the Old and New Testaments (Isaiah 9:7; Luke 1:32).

Cultic usage: the television show called *Key of David* is hosted by Gerald Flurry, the author of a book of the same name. Flurry is the founder and pastor of the Philadelphia Church of God. His interpretations of Scripture include the twisting of many biblical prophecies and a reading of many other passages as being secretly prophetic.

Flurry has a special interest in Revelation 3:7–13, the letter to the church at Philadelphia (the ancient city located in modern-day Turkey). Flurry claims that the Key of David held by Christ is "the profound understanding he wants all of us to have" (*Key of David*, p.10), which will lead to special "positions of authority" (p. 11) in the New Jerusalem. Flurry claims that the letter is a vision of what Christians of our time are to do, but that "only a small percentage" (p. 8) will understand this great vision, qualify to receive the special authority, and share the throne of David with Jesus.

Another major component of Flurry's beliefs is the claim that Great Britain and the United States of America (meaning their Caucasian, Anglo-Saxon citizens) are descended from the *lost* tribes of Israel. As Israelites (he says), we are uniquely qualified to hold authority in the kingdom and create the spiritual Israel. This belief in Anglo-Israelism has no basis in fact.

Conclusion: Paul told Timothy to avoid *myths* and endless genealogies. These promote controversies rather than God's work—"which is by faith" (1 Tim. 1:4). There is no "special knowledge" beyond the gospel itself that will aid salvation. Any claim beyond faith in the work of Jesus tears out the heart of the good news: that the just will live by faith (Rom. 1:17). There is no great vision, special knowledge, or Jewish lineage needed, only faith in Christ.

The second attempt to define the Key of David was made by Port Austin Bible Center. They appear to be associated with Gerald Flurry's Philadelphia Church of God. The following is their definition for this divine key as posted on gotquestions.org:

> Question: What is the Key of David?
>
> Answer: Used twice in Scripture (Isa. 22:22; Rev. 3:7), the phrase "Key of David" refers to processing legitimate authority to rule Israel, the hold nation of God. The Key of David doesn't refer to a physical throne or to a physical nation. Israel is the woman of Revelation chapter 12. She goes from being the physical nation that gave birth to Christ Jesus (verse 5) to the spiritual nation whose offspring keep the commandments of God and hold the testimony of Jesus (verse 17), which is the spirit of prophesy (Rev. 19:10). Israel will become the single great nation promised to the patriarch Abraham (Gen.12:2) when the kingdom of the world becomes the kingdom of the Most High and of His Christ (Rev. 11:15–18; Daniel 7:8–14).

But the Key of David means more than who has the right to rule Israel. The Key of David is the key that unlocks Scripture. It means understanding the writings (Psalms) of King David, the man after God's heart, a man who used the outside/inside movement of Hebraic poetics to simultaneously reveal and conceal knowledge. David's use of repetition to form couplets within David's songs, a poetic style he inherited, visible to the invisible, thereby causing the visible to become a copy and shadow of the invisible (Heb. 8:5 et al).

In addition to the two foregoing attempts to answer this question, I decided to include an interesting response from biblestudy.org whose response to this question lines up with what both Prophet Ellis has stated and what Jesus himself has thus stated. That is, no man knows about this hidden manna and white stone, but he who has received it (Rev. 3:17). The response from biblestudy.org states as follows:

> Question: What is the Key of David, and what does it symbolize?
>
> Answer: What you are referring to only appears once in the Bible, "To the angel of the church in Philadelphia write...who holds the KEY OF DAVID" (Rev. 3:7). The speaker is the resurrected Jesus, whom John sees in a vision, and the message is to the church at Philadelphia. Unfortunately, Scripture is silent regarding a direct answer to your question. There is a lot of conjecture and supposition on this subject, but one should understand that the Bible does not specifically identify this object.

The one thing that made David unique was the promise God made to him. God, speaking through the prophet Jeremiah, prophesied of the descendent who would bring salvation and confirm His covenant with all.

The Lord said, "The time is coming when I will fulfill the promise that I made to the people of Israel and Judah. At that time I will choose as king a righteous descendant of David. That king will do what is right and just throughout the land...I will choose one of David's descendants to rule over the descendants of Abraham, Isaac, and Jacob. I will be merciful to my people and make them prosperous again" (Jer. 33:14–15, 26).

Some have speculated that the covenant would require a physical descendent to be ruling over at least some portion of Israel down to our present time. One explanation of this can be found in *Judah's Sceptre and Joseph's Birthright* written by J. H. Allen. He makes a powerful case for the lineage of rulers existing today.

The problem with considering this to be a physical ruling king of the present time is that the covenant also covered the Levites (Jer. 33:18). We know that since the time Jesus became our High Priest, the Levitical priesthood has had no function (see Hebrews 7–10). Some have explained this problem by saying that Jesus, a descendant of King David through Mary, now rules over "spiritual Israel," the church, and will in the future once again physically rule over Israel on this earth. That still does not explain the question of the promise of the Levitical priesthood remaining functioning and offering burnt offerings and sacrifices.

A key was often worn on the shoulder of those who possessed official authority and power (see Isaiah 22). In the New Testament, they were also symbolic of these traits. In Revelation, Jesus is said to have several of them which unlock death and Hades (or the grave, see Revelation 1:18). An angel, also in Revelation, is given one to lock the spiritual cell or "bottomless pit" where a bound Satan will be constrained for one thousand years (Rev. 20:1). This evidence points to this object representing, at least figuratively, the possession of power and has nothing whatsoever to do with Biblical prophecy.

Thankfully, Jesus and His apostles have given us the plan for our salvation, and that salvation does not depend on the Key of David and our interpretation of what it is. It is, indeed, one of the most fascinating areas of study in the Bible, but we should not claim to know for certain what this means. Each of us will have to decide for himself the spiritual meaning of this object. (Unquote)

It should be clear that the Key of David is something that has remained secret to be revealed at an appointed time. I will show that the Key of David is of such divine and spiritual nature when revealed, it proves itself as being the genuine and correct definition. The authoritative answer and definition for the Key of David provided by Prophet Ellis is this:

Answer from Prophet Ellis: The Key of David is the substance of two candlestick-shaped stone pillars, each being identical in size, whose height stands exactly 69.375 feet tall so that its height may act as a key to many divine-locked doors. The stones were hewed out of a great mountain without hands but by the Spirit of God (Dan. 2:44–47). The stone, as it is described in verses 30 and 47 of the second chapter of Daniel, has remained a secret. Thus, it could not have been defined by man. God hid these two candlestick-shaped stone pillars at the entry to Pharaoh's house in Egypt (Jer. 43:7–13). They would serve as a token for his end-time messenger whom he called the branch (Zech. 3:8–9). God will send the branch of David to come forth and build His temple (Zech. 6:12).

No man in the earth knows where the original seven golden candlestick pillars of Israel are hidden. Only the height of the two candlesticks that God calls his two witnesses in Revelation 11:1–19 can be used as a key to finding them, and only by the Spirit of God. God has hidden seven golden candlesticks in the earth to symbolize the power and authority that He has given to the seven leading industrialized nations. These nations refer to themselves as the G7.

Prophet Ellis went to Moscow, Russia, just three months after the fall of the Soviet Union to prepare for the coming of the G8. Russia joined the G7 to become the G8 after the fall of the Soviet Union. This accounts for what Israel calls the eight golden candlesticks. This candlestick is the same stone or rock that the Spirit of God revealed to Peter so that He would know Jesus as the Son of God (Matt. 16:13–19). This stone is the key to many things including the kingdom of heaven. This candlestick stone pillar represents the power Christ has given to both the nations and the churches.

In his message to the angel of the church at Ephesus, Christ reminded him as follows, saying, "Remember therefore from whence thou art fallen, and repent, and do the first works; or else I will come unto thee quickly, and will remove thy candlestick out of his place, except thou repent."

These two candlestick stone pillars are commonly called Cleopatra's Needles. They are symbolized in earth by the two needlepoints on the master mason compass and square, which they refer to as their cornerstone. This is because the Revelation of this stone by God's messenger acts as a signal to rebuild God's temple that he described in Ezekiel chapters 40 through chapter 48. The building of this temple which both the G7/G8 nations now oppose is their obligation for God's favors toward them. The favoritism that God has shown to the United States is confirmed by the Latin phrase *annuit coeptis* found on the US one-dollar bill with the US Great Seal. The dollar bill was designed to conceal the seven golden candlesticks, which embodies the twelve memorial stones of Israel's exodus from Egypt. The English translation for the Latin phrase *annuit coeptis* is "fortune" (God, if you must) has favored (or smiled upon) our undertakings.

Our nation's first president and fifty-three of the signers of the Declaration of Independence were Freemasons. The Freemasons recognize that these two candlestick pillars, which God hid at the entry of Pharaoh's house, would be used to identify God's messenger by his knowledge of this hidden keystone. In order to circumvent this, the ruling powers of Egypt, who were Islamic Freemasons, would give these two candlestick stone pillars to the west. The New York Metropolitan Museum of Art has published a seventy-two-page book, which chronicles the great task of moving these two pillars from Egypt to the west. The book is titled *The New York Obelisk* or *How Cleopatra's Needle Came to New York and What Happened When It Got Here*.

In 1877, the first pillar would be moved to London where it stands today on the banks of London's River Thames. In 1880, its twin would be moved to New York Central Park where it stands today. Page 42 of the book states on October 9, 1880, a parade of nine thousand Freemasons marched up Fifth Avenue, bands blaring to Greywacke Knoll for a grand and solemn cornerstone ceremony.

After having moved these two candlesticks from the place God openly stated they were hidden, the Freemasons and the nations were confident that God's messenger would not find them.

Just as God revealed the mystery of this stone to Peter by His Sprit, He would likewise, by His Spirit, reveal to Prophet Ellis where the seven golden candlesticks are hidden. It's a revelation supported by scripture whereby God moves His dialogue on this stone in Zechariah 3:8–9 and continues it in Zechariah 4. There the stone become seven candlesticks revealed by God's Spirit to His messenger. It states as follows:

> And the angel that talked with me came again, and waked me, as a man that is wakened out of his sleep. And said unto me, What seest thou? And I said, I have looked, and behold a candlestick all of gold, with a bowl upon the top of it, and his seven lamps thereon, and seven pipes to the seven lamps, which are upon the top thereof: And two olive trees by it, one upon the right side of the bowl, and the other upon the left side thereof.
>
> So I answered and spake to the angel that talked with me, saying, What are these, my lord? Then the angel that talked with me answered and said unto me, Knowest thou not what these be? And I said, No, my lord. Then he answered and spake unto me, saying, This is the word of the Lord unto Zerubbabel, saying, Not by might, nor by power, but by my spirit, saith the Lord of hosts. Who art thou, O great mountain? before Zerubbabel thou shalt become a plain: and he shall bring forth the

headstone thereof with shoutings, crying, Grace, grace unto it. Moreover the word of the Lord came unto me, saying, The hands of Zerubbabel have laid the foundation of this house; his hands shall also finish it; and thou shalt know that the Lord of hosts hath sent me unto you. For who hath despised the day of small things? for they shall rejoice, and shall see the plummet in the hand of Zerubbabel with those seven; they are the eyes of the Lord, which run to and fro through the whole earth. Then answered I, and said unto him, What are these two olive trees upon the right side of the candlestick and upon the left side thereof? And I answered again, and said unto him, What be these two olive branches which through the two golden pipes empty the golden oil out of themselves? And he answered me and said, Knowest thou not what these be? And I said, No, my lord. Then said he, These are the two anointed ones, that stand by the Lord of the whole earth. (Zech. 4:1–14)

All the questions that were put forth to Zechariah were answered *no*. This is because of the mysteries that hid these great stones as the seven golden candlesticks. God will reveal the mystery by his Spirit.

After moving this stone candlestick pillar to New York Central Park in 1880, the Freemasons would begin that same year constructing the Washington Memorial. It would be constructed in the same form and shape as Cleopatra's Needles for the G7/G8 nations that were to come. The memorial would be constructed to rise 8 times 69.375 feet for a total height of 555 feet for the seven golden candlesticks plus one for Russia's new membership. Thus, this stone is a key that opens a golden door to the seven golden candlesticks of Israel. It is, therefore, rightly called a keystone by those who embrace it.

By comparing the best answers among the four answers for "what is the Key of David," I have concluded that only Prophet Ellis's answer is correct and authoritative. His answer defining the Key of David is expanded in all the following chapters of my thesis. In doing so, this key unlocks the mystery of the golden oil, which Zechariah saw being emptied out of the candlestick's golden pipe. This is the crude oil which has empowered US Commerce and the commerce of the G7/G8 leading industrialized nations. Unlocking doors like these confirms that this key actually works.

Notes

Related References: Freemasonry Bibles Progressive Steps in Masonry for the 16° (XVI) "Prince of Jerusalem". We no longer expect to rebuild the Temple of Jerusalem. To us it has become but a symbol. To us the whole world is God's Temple, as is every upright heart. To establish all over the world the New Law and Reign of Love, Peace, Charity, and Toleration, is to build that Temple, most acceptable to God, in erecting which Masonry is now engaged.

No longer needing to repair to Jerusalem to worship, nor to offer up sacrifices and shed blood to propitiate the Deity, man may make the woods and mountains his Churches and Temples, and worship God with a devout gratitude and with works of charity and beneficence to his fellow-men. Wherever the humble and contrite heart silently offers up its adoration, under the overarching trees, in the open, level meadows, on the hill-side, in the glen, or in the city's swarming street; there is God's House and the New Jerusalem.

Related references: The staff of John Hagee Ministries evaluates Prophet Ellis' manuscript "Upon This Rock" in their letter dated April 18, 2009 to Prophet Ellis, saying: Dear Prophet Ellis, Members of our staff at John Hagee Ministries reviewed your letter describing your research and the insight and revelations given to you by God. It is obvious that you have a good understanding of the history and spiritual issues concerning the Masonic Order. Thank you for providing Pastor Hagee with your manuscript entitled "Upon This Rock". We praise God for your faithfulness in the work of the Kingdom.

Excerpts from Prophet Ellis' prophetic diary, whereby, the Angel of the Lord speaks to him on the stone and the Key of David:

May 17, 1999 at 2:00 A.M., the Holy Spirit speaks saying, "This white stone will become a sectional bible."

December 27, 2004 at 12:00 A.M., the Holy Spirit speaks saying, "The power of this stone is a Key that will open many doors".

January 2, 2008 at 3:20 A.M., the angel of the Lord speaks saying, "The purpose of this key is to go forth and complete the work of God."

January 2, 2008 at 4:40 A.M., the angel of the Lord speaks saying, "The Lord has given you power to come forth and prepare the place of His rest."

Chapter 3

The Washington Monument Is Certified as the Seven Golden Candlesticks plus One for the G8

All Masonic Bibles are printed with the two centerpieces of Freemasonry inside of them. These two centerpieces are the Washington Memorial and the George Washington Masonic apron. Section 3 deals with the Washington Monument and its certification, as eight golden candlesticks joined together as a white stone pillar. The Washington Monument, as it appears in Masonic Bibles, will be illustrated on my following page. All the graphics appearing with it are uniquely positioned to convert plain biblical text into complex symbolism, which cannot be read by neither Freemasons nor nonFreemasons. There may be some exceptions to a small number of high ranking Freemasons, but the average Freemason is not given the order's ultimate secrets. Such secrets must come by the revelations of God as they have to Prophet Ellis.

On the following page, I will illustrate how the graphics accompanying the monument covert the plain biblical text of Revelation 1:12–14 and Zechariah 4:1–14 into symbolism. Revelation 1:12–14 is a story of Christ appearing to John in a vision with hair white as snow walking in the middle of seven golden candlesticks. This vision is converted into symbolism by placing George Washington, whose hair was white as snow, in the middle of the Washington Monument. By doing so, he is in the midst of seven golden candlesticks. However, the eyes only see one because they are all joined together. When the angel tested Zechariah to determine if he could recognize something that should have been very familiar to him, Zachariah answered *no* each time. He had eyes, but he could not see.

At the base of the candlestick are two olive trees. One is on the right side, and the other is on the left side as written in Zechariah 4:1–14. Yet there is much more conversion of biblical text into symbolism.

It is not coincidental that the book of Revelation begins with the appearance of Christ walking through the midst of seven golden candlesticks. This is because it is these seven golden candlesticks, which holds the biggest secrets, and thus reveal Jesus Christ by unlocking the greatest secrets in both the Bible and the earth. John begins his account of one of the Bible's greatest vision with these words:

> I John, who also am your brother, and companion in tribulation, and in the kingdom and patience of Jesus Christ, was in the isle that is called Patmos, for the word of God, and for the testimony of Jesus Christ. I was in the Spirit on the Lord's day, and heard behind me a great voice, as of a trumpet, Saying, I am Alpha and Omega, the first and the last: and, What thou seest, write in a book, and send it unto the seven churches which are in Asia; unto Ephesus, and unto Smyrna, and unto Pergamos, and unto Thyatira, and unto Sardis, and unto Philadelphia, and unto Laodicea.
>
> And I turned to see the voice that spake with me. And being turned, I saw seven golden candlesticks; And in the midst of the seven candlesticks one like unto the Son of man, clothed with a garment down to the foot, and girt about the paps with a golden girdle. His head and his hairs were white like wool, as white as snow; and his eyes were as a flame of fire; And his feet like unto fine brass, as if they burned in a furnace; and his voice as the sound of many waters. And he had in his right hand seven stars: and out of his mouth went a sharp two edged sword: and his countenance was as the

sun shineth in his strength. And when I saw him, I fell at his feet as dead. And he laid his right hand upon me, saying unto me, Fear not; I am the first and the last:

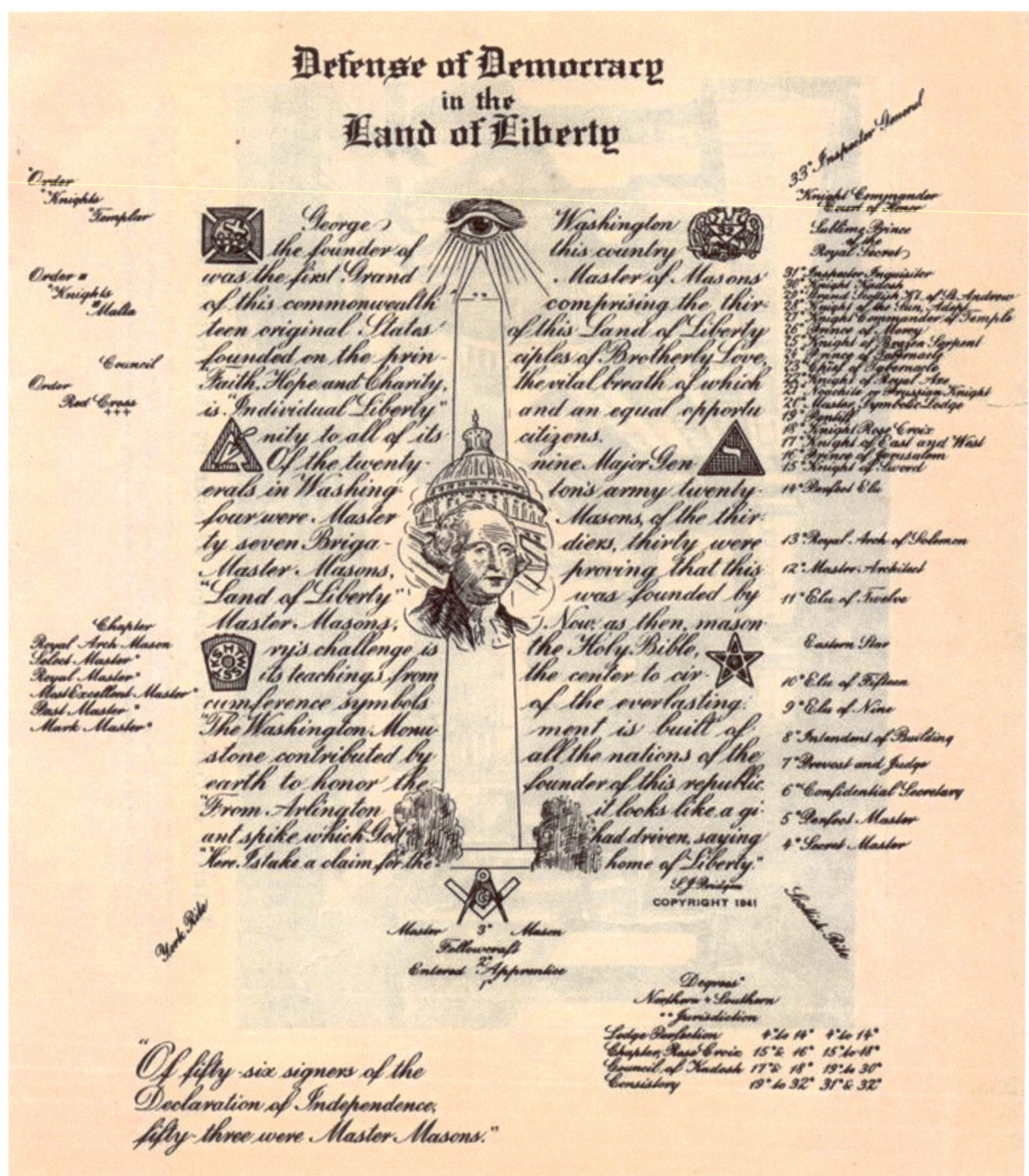

I am he that liveth, and was dead; and, behold, I am alive for evermore, Amen; and have the keys of hell and of death. Write the things which thou hast seen, and the things which are, and the things which shall be hereafter; The mystery of the seven stars which thou sawest in my right hand, and the seven golden candlesticks. The seven stars are the angels of the seven churches: and the seven candlesticks which thou sawest are the seven churches. (Rev. 1:9–20)

A mystery is a divine truth that is made known only by the revelation of God. It is a secret and cannot be uncovered by intellect or research.

The revelations given by God to Prophet Ellis have thereafter been confirmed and proven by spiritually guided research. Example: the angels of the seven churches are referred to as *stars*. These stars are a secret society of stars that have fallen from heaven with Satan into the earth. These stars are Masonry and their eastern stars. They are the one-thirds of those stars that were cast out of heaven with Satan. This one-thirds became known as the 33-degree emblem of Freemasonry because one-thirds is 33% of 100. The 33-degree emblem of Freemasonry is a nine-pointed star. The eastern star emblem has the word *fatal* written thereon to symbolize death. Jesus left a code of these fallen angels inside the church when he reminded the angel of the church at Ephesus to remember from where he had fallen. This angel was in a church where there were evil, false apostles, and liars. Therefore, Jesus sent a message saying as follows:

> Unto the angel of the church of Ephesus write; These things saith he that holdeth the seven stars in his right hand, who walketh in the midst of the seven golden candlesticks; I know thy works, and thy labour, and thy patience, and how thou canst not bear them which are evil: and thou hast tried them which say they are apostles, and are not, and hast found them liars: And hast borne, and hast patience, and for my name's sake hast laboured, and hast not fainted. Nevertheless I have somewhat against thee, because thou hast left thy first love. Remember therefore from whence thou art fallen, and repent, and do the first works; or else I will come unto thee quickly, and will remove thy candlestick out of his place, except thou repent. (Rev. 2:1–5)

Ephesus was the first of the seven churches addressed, and therefore, it held the key to the mysteries of all the others. These are the stars that fell from heaven. It is both a wonder and a mystery now revealed.

> And there appeared another wonder in heaven; and behold a great red dragon, having seven heads and ten horns, and seven crowns upon his heads. And his tail drew the third part of the stars of heaven, and did cast them to the earth: and the dragon stood before the woman which was ready to be delivered, for to devour her child as soon as it was born. And there was war in heaven: Michael and his angels fought against the dragon; and the dragon fought and his angels, And prevailed not; neither was their place found any more in heaven. And the great dragon was cast out, that old serpent, called the Devil, and Satan, which deceiveth the whole world: he was cast out into the earth, and his angels were cast out with him. Therefore rejoice, ye heavens, and ye that dwell in them. Woe to the inhabiters of the earth and of the sea! for the devil is come down unto you, having great wrath, because he knoweth that he hath but a short time. (Rev. 12:3–4, 7–9, 12)

These stars would become the chief ensign for the gentile nations.

> And in that day there shall be a root of Jesse, which shall stand for an ensign of the people; to it shall the Gentiles seek: and his rest shall be glorious. (Isa. 11:10)

Additional biblical texts were converted to symbolism that will certify the Washington Monument as a candlestick. The Capitol rotunda, which is shaped as a round bushel, is placed symbolically over the candlestick along next to Washington's image. The reflection pool built in front of the monument was designed to cast two candlesticks placing one under water as under a bed. It was a conversion of the words spoken by Jesus in Mark 4:21–23 regarding this mystery. Mark wrote as follows:

> And he said unto them, Is a candle brought to be put under a bushel, or under a bed? and not to be set on a candlestick? For there is nothing hid, which shall not be manifested; neither was any thing kept secret, but that it should come abroad. If any man have ears to hear, let him hear. (Mark 4:21–23)

Another conversion was achieved by placing the master mason compass and square beneath the monument as a pillow. This emblem is called a cornerstone. When they place it at the base of the monument as a pillow, it allows this cornerstone to be symbolically raised as a pillar. This is a conversion of the plain biblical text of Genesis 28:18 where Jacob put this stone for his pillow at Bethel and raised it as a pillar.

> And Jacob rose up early in the morning, and took the stone that he had put for his pillows, and set it up for a pillar, and poured oil upon the top of it. And he called the name of that place Bethel: but the name of that city was called Luz at the first. And this stone, which I have set for a pillar, shall be God's house: and of all that thou shalt give me I will surely give the tenth unto thee. (Gen. 28:18–19, 22)

This pillar, which Jacob said shall be God's house, is the candlestick that Jesus said is the seven churches. Thus, the mystery is revealed certifying this stone as a candlestick.

Notes

> Matthew Henry's Concise Commentary regarding God's Two Candlestick and Two Olive Tree Witnesses: Revelation 11:1–13. In the time of treading down, God kept his faithful witnesses to attest the truth of his word and worship, and the excellence of his ways. The number of these witnesses is small, yet enough. They prophesy in sackcloth. It shows their afflicted, persecuted state, and deep sorrow for the abominations against which they protested. They are supported during their great and hard work, till it is done. When they had prophesied in sackcloth the greatest part of 1260 days, antichrist, the great instrument of the devil, would war against them, with force and violence for a time. Determined rebels against the light rejoice, as on some happy event, when they can silence, drive to a distance, or destroy the faithful servants of Christ, whose doctrine and conduct torment them. It does not appear that the term is yet expired, and the witnesses are not at present exposed to endure such terrible outward suffering as in former times; but such things may again happen, and there is abundant cause to prophesy in sackcloth, on account of the state of religion.

> The depressed state of real Christianity may relate only to the western church. The Spirit of life from God, quickens the dead souls, and shall quicken the dead bodies of his people, and his dying interest in the world. The revival of God's work and witnesses, will strike terror into the souls of his enemies. Where there is guilt, there is fear, and a persecuting spirit, though cruel, is a cowardly spirit. It will be no small part of the punishment of persecutors, both

in this world, and at the great day, that they see the faithful servants of God honored and advanced. The Lord's witnesses must not be weary of suffering and service, nor must stay till their Master calls them. The consequences of their being thus exalted was a might shock and convulsion in the antichristian empire. Events alone can show the meaning of this. But whenever God's work and witnesses revive, the devil's work and witnesses fall before him. And that the slaying of the witnesses is future appears to be probable.

Related Commentary from biblehub.com Pulpit Commentary: These are the two olive trees, and the two candlesticks. The "two olive trees" and the "two candlesticks" are here identical. Thus, while John uses the figure of Zechariah, he does not apply it in every detail. In the prophet, but one candlestick is mentioned. "The two olive trees" which supply the material for the candlesticks, are from emblem of the Old and New Testaments: the candlesticks typify the Jewish and Christian churches. These are identical so far as being God's witnesses; the Church derives her stores from the Word of God is manifested through the Church.

Standing before the God of the earth; (The Lord of the earth). The participles is masculine, though the preceding article and nouns are feminine, probably as being more in keeping with the masculine character under which the two witnesses are depicted. Perhaps he is described as the "Lord of the earth", since the witnesses are to prophesy before all the earth. (cf. verse 9 and Mathew 24:14)

Chapter 4

The Purpose of the Key of David

Entries made by Prophet Ellis into his diary on January 2, 2008, confirm that the angel of the Lord gave him the specific purpose of this key. In an entry made at 10:42 p.m. on January 1, 2008, the angel of the Lord spoke to Prophet Ellis, saying, "I say this with three emotions—the spirit of love, the spirit of hope, and the spirit of forgiveness." The next entries into his diary came nearly four hours later. It was then on January 2, 2008, when the angel of the Lord gave Prophet Ellis in simple words the purpose of this keystone. "The purpose of this key is to go forth and complete the work of God."

The angel of the Lord appeared again unto Prophet Ellis at 4:40 a.m., saying, "The Lord has given you power to come forth to prepare the place of his rest." The diary of Prophet Ellis also shows that the angel of the Lord appeared unto him on April 12, 2003, at 4:18 a.m. and said unto him, "Name your stone." Prophet Ellis replied in the Spirit, saying, "Bethel." The angel immediately responded, saying, "Thou has received a blessing." At 5:16 a.m., Prophet Ellis saw heaven open according to entries made into his diary.

It is apparent that the genealogy and Semitic background of Afro-Americans have been buried and hidden beneath the veils that cover slavery and history. For this reason, the angel of the Lord appeared to Prophet Ellis on September 1, 2003, at 11:20 p.m. with this message, saying, "Until the truth and the true picture is learned about blacks, who they are and how they got here, hardship shall remain until the day of death."

This keystone is also the rod that was promised in both Revelation 11:1 and Isaiah 11:1. This rod is now working for the kingdom of God.

Jesus realized the purpose of this stone and why all references to it should be by dark sentences, codes, and parables. He spoke a parable to the chief priests and Pharisees concerning this stone relationship to the kingdom of God, which would be taken from them. Suspecting that he knew the mystery of this stone, they sought to kill him, but they feared the multitude because they took him for a prophet. Matthew wrote this following account in his gospel.

> They say unto him, He will miserably destroy those wicked men, and will let out his vineyard unto other husbandmen, which shall render him the fruits in their seasons.
>
> Therefore say I unto you, The kingdom of God shall be taken from you, and given to a nation bringing forth the fruits thereof. And whosoever shall fall on this stone shall be broken: but on whomsoever it shall fall, it will grind him to powder.
>
> And when the chief priests and Pharisees had heard his parables, they perceived that he spake of them. But when they sought to lay hands on him, they feared the multitude, because they took him for a prophet. (Matt. 21:41, 43–46)

This prophesy by Jesus, which the kingdom of God shall be taken from those ruling powers in the earth, is corroborated not only from Daniel's interpretation of Nebuchadnezzar's dream of this stone, it is also corroborated by John's account in Revelation of the death and resurrection of God's two candlesticks witnesses. This confirms that the candlestick and the stones are the same. John writes the following account of the stone candlesticks which God calls His two witnesses.

> And I will give power unto my two witnesses, and they shall prophesy a thousand two hundred and threescore days, clothed in sackcloth. These are the two olive trees, and the two candlesticks standing before the God of the earth. (Rev. 11:3–4)

When Daniel interpreted Nebuchadnezzar's dream about this stone, he revealed that he would essentially be god of the whole earth in the last days when God established his throne upon these hidden stones. These were the two candlestick stone pillars that John saw standing before the God of the whole earth. A capital *G* is used in the scripture so that it may conceal that which would come by revelation. In order to establish the king of Babylon's throne upon these stones, then God must raise him up from the bottomless pit to receive his kingdom. Therefore, John continued describing his revelation that was signified to him on the isle of Patmos by the angel of the Lord.

> And when they shall have finished their testimony, the beast that ascendeth out of the bottomless pit shall make war against them, and shall overcome them, and kill them. And their dead bodies shall lie in the street of the great city, which spiritually is called Sodom and Egypt, where also our Lord was crucified. (Rev. 11:7–8)

This city that is spiritually called Sodom and Egypt alludes to the city where these two candlesticks stand today after they were removed from Egypt. The first was moved from Egypt in 1877 to the banks of the River Thames in London, where it remains standing today. Its twin was moved in 1880 to New York Central Park where it remains standing today. That same year, construction would begin on the Washington Monument, and the United States would adopt Egyptian emblems as its seal. It would then become spiritual Sodom and Egypt where God's two witnesses shall be killed.

Jesus spoke to the chief priests and the Pharisees in Matthew 21:41–46, a parable alluding to the relationship between this stone and the kingdom of God. Joshua confirmed that this stone shall be a witness unto Israel, lest it deny its God. God has called His two witnesses the two candlesticks, which are two stone pillars. The fulfillment of Jesus's prophesy, saying the kingdom of God shall be taken from those who fall on this stone, is confirmed by John's vision of the death and resurrection of the two candlestick witnesses.

> And they of the people and kindreds and tongues and nations shall see their dead bodies three days and an half, and shall not suffer their dead bodies to be put in graves. And they that dwell upon the earth shall rejoice over them, and make merry, and shall send gifts one to another; because these two prophets tormented them that dwelt on the earth.
>
> And after three days and an half the spirit of life from God entered into them, and they stood upon their feet; and great fear fell upon them which saw them. And they heard a great voice from heaven saying unto them, Come up hither. And they ascended up to heaven in a cloud; and their enemies beheld them. And the same hour was there a great earthquake, and the tenth part of the city fell, and in the earthquake were slain of men seven thousand: and the remnant were affrighted, and gave glory to the God of heaven. The second woe is past; and, behold, the third woe cometh quickly.
>
> And the seventh angel sounded; and there were great voices in heaven, saying, The kingdoms of this world are become the kingdoms of our Lord, and of his Christ; and he shall reign for ever and ever. And the nations were angry, and thy wrath is come, and the time of the dead, that they should be judged. (Rev. 11:9–15, 18)

Notes

RELATED SOURCES: Freemason Bible Copyright 1971 "The John A. Hertel Co." Biblical Index To Freemasonry page 36. "Signet of Zerubbabel", (Haggai 2:23) A special token given to Zerubbabel by the Lord as a sign of his divine call to rebuild the Temple of God at Jerusalem.

NOTE: Zerubbabel was the anointed Prince, and a BRANCH of King David. He lead the delegation who returned from Babylonian captivity to rebuild the second Temple. Page 39 in the Biblical Index To Freemasonry write the following about him:

ZERUBBABEL: Zerubbabel was a notable character intimately associated in a symbolic manner with the degrees of Royal Arch Masonry and other higher degrees. Born in Babylon as a Jewish exile, he was later appointed first governor of Judea by King Cyrus. He led in rebuilding the Temple at Jerusalem.

NOTE: Prince Zerubbabel is the focus of the 16° degree of the Progressive Steps In Freemasonry found on page 16 which degree is title "Prince of Jerusalem". This degree states as follows:

"We no longer expect to rebuild the Temple at Jerusalem. To us it has become but a symbol. To us the whole world is GOD's TEMPLE, AS IS every upright heart. To establish all over the world the New Law and Reign of Love, Peace, Charity, and Toleration, is to build that Temple, most acceptable to God, in erecting which Masonry is now engaged. No longer needing to repair to Jerusalem to worship, or to offer up sacrifices and shed blood to propitiate the Deity, man may make the woods and mountains his Churches and Temples, and worship God with a devout gratitude with works of charity and beneficence to his fellow-men. Wherever the humble and contrite heart silently offers up its adoration, under the overarching trees, in the open, level meadows, on the hill-side, in the glen, or in the city's swarming street; there is God's House and the New Jerusalem."

White Stone (p.39) The white stone is a token of fraternal friendship and helpfulness, or endearing alliance.

COVENANT OF MASONS: (P.28) A covenant is a contract or agreement between two or more parties on certain terms. In becoming a Mason, a man enters into a covenant with the Fraternity, agreeing to fulfill certain promises and perform certain duties. On the other hand, the Fraternity and its members bind themselves to certain ties of friendship, brotherliness, protection, support, and benefits. The breaking of a covenant is subject to stated penalties; The Masonic covenant includes specific penalties.

Obligation (P.34) From time immemorial, men have entered into covenants of brotherhood and friendship under solemn oaths of fidelity and loyalty, and whenever the circumstances and purpose justified it, secrecy has been pledged. This practice among Masons has many precedents and is based upon the truths and principles of the Great Light of Masonry. The oath in such covenants is given in the name of God; perjury in such oaths is subject to severe and deadly penalties. All vows voluntarily taken in Masonry must be faithfully performed and are never subject to revocation.

Chapter 5

Two Candlestick Keystones Certified as a Rod for Measuring and Identifying the Seven Golden Candlesticks

The precise size 69.375 feet of Cleopatra's Needles allows them to be referred to in the Bible as a measuring rod given to God's two witnesses as a token to rebuild His temple. In other words, as confirmed by Prophet Ellis, this term measuring rod is used to identify something that is secret. That secret is the seven golden candlesticks, which can be found and identified only with this unique measuring reed. It is represented, as I have shown earlier, by the master mason compass and square, which is a precise measuring instrument.

> And there was given me a reed like unto a rod: and the angel stood, saying, Rise, and measure the temple of God, and the altar, and them that worship therein. (Rev. 11:1)

I will use the graphics on my following page taken from a Masonic Bible to *prove* just how Cleopatra's Needles were encrypted into the Bible as a measuring reed. To prove this, it must be recalled that the two needlepoints on the master mason's compass symbolize Cleopatra's Needles, which are the two candlesticks known as God's two witnesses. To measure the altar as mentioned in the foregoing Revelation 11:1, the masons would simply place their compass on a Bible, lying upon an altar between two candlesticks, inside a temple with seven golden candlesticks. All these things are the subject of the Masonic graphics on my following page. These graphics simply convert the plain biblical text from Revelation 11:1–4 into complex Masonic symbolism.

This measuring reed is called a golden reed because it identifies the seven golden candlesticks and the city that is called New Jerusalem. A city whose foundation is built upon these twelve precious stones, which have been raised as a pillar.

> Him that overcometh will I make a pillar in the temple of my God, and he shall go no more out: and I will write upon him the name of my God, and the name of the city of my God, which is new Jerusalem, which cometh down out of heaven from my God: and I will write upon him my new name. (Rev. 3:12)

Now the golden reed is used to measure the city.

> And he carried me away in the spirit to a great and high mountain, and shewed me that great city, the holy Jerusalem, descending out of heaven from God, And he that talked with me had a golden reed to measure the city, and the gates thereof, and the wall thereof. And the city lieth foursquare, and the length is as large as the breadth: and he measured the city with the reed, twelve thousand furlongs. The length and the breadth and the height of it are equal.

> And the foundations of the wall of the city were garnished with all manner of precious stones. The first foundation was jasper; the second, sapphire; the third, a chalcedony; the fourth, an emerald; The fifth, sardonyx; the sixth, sardius; the seventh, chrysolyte; the eighth, beryl; the ninth, a topaz; the tenth, a chrysoprasus; the eleventh, a jacinth; the twelfth, an amethyst. (Rev. 21:10, 15–16, 19–20)

This New Jerusalem has been confirmed by Prophet Ellis as New York City. This is the city where Cleopatra's Needle was brought to signify that which John would prophesy.

Jesus spoke prophesies in parables in the gospels of Mark and Matthew, concerning this measuring reed, the city, and the candlestick whose light shall reveal the city New Jerusalem. First, the candle and the measuring line shall be illustrated from Jesus's prophesy in Mark's gospel.

> And he said unto them, Is a candle brought to be put under a bushel, or under a bed? and not to be set on a candlestick? For there is nothing hid, which shall not be manifested; neither was any thing kept secret, but that it should come abroad. If any man have ears to hear, let him hear. And he said unto them, Take heed what ye hear: with what measure ye mete, it shall be measured to you: and unto you that hear shall more be given. (Mark 4:21–24)

Next, Jesus speaks a parable concerning New Jerusalem, a city that sits on a hill and could not be hid but is searched and found by the light of a candle. This parable was part of his great sermon that was preached on the mount.

> Ye are the light of the world. A city that is set on an hill cannot be hid. Neither do men light a candle, and put it under a bushel, but on a candlestick; and it giveth light unto all that are in the house. (Matt. 5:14–15)

In perhaps, what is the most profound prophesy that describes New Jerusalem being found by the mystery of the seven golden candlesticks is spoken by the prophet Zephaniah. Zephaniah prophesied of God's judgment of both Judah and all nations. In these, he mentioned Jerusalem will be searched with candles in that great day when God shall execute judgment.

> And it shall come to pass at that time, that I will search Jerusalem with candles, and punish the men that are settled on their lees: that say in their heart, The Lord will not do good, neither will he do evil. (Zeph. 1:12)

The Cleopatra Needle stone candlestick has been standing in New York for some 135 years symbolically as candles searching Jerusalem. The light atop the Washington Monument, as the seven golden candlesticks, has also symbolically been searching and measuring the city New Jerusalem.

Notes

REFERENCES: The New York History of an Egyptians Obelisk—Nytimes.com May 29, 2014. At 220 tons, Cleopatra's Needle appears to be the heaviest pieces of stone brought into Manhattan since the time of the glaciers. Its journey in 1880 from Alexandria to America was routine, but its progress from the Hudson River at West 96th to Central Park was one of the sights of New York.

Thutmose III was in the fourth decade of his reign when, in 1443 B.C., he commissioned two obelisks, quarried at Aswan and floated down the Nile to the capital at Heliopolis. There they remained until around 10 B. C., when the Romans concluded they would be best sited at Alexandria. The term Cleopatra's Needle was in use no later than 1869, when Mark Twain used it in his book "The Innocents Abroad," although it is doubtful the obelisks had any relationship to the Egyptian queen.

The British wrangled an obelisk from Egypt in 1878, and set it up in London, so it was not remarkable that New York sought to rival the British capital. William Henry Hurbert, the editor of the New York World, was surely thinking of American prestige when he began a campaign to acquire an obelisk around the same time, although the possibilities of newspaper sales no doubt stimulated his patriotism.

There were some delays, Egyptian nationalists objected to sending the nation's patrimony overseas, and a creditor of the Egyptian government threatened to place a lien on the obelisk. But Egypt signed ownership over to the United States in 1879. The New York Times remarked sourly, "There is no longer any hope that we shall escape the Alexandria obelisk."

In charge of the trans-ATLANTIC VOYAGE WAS A Navy officer on furlough, Lt. Cmdr. Henry Gorringe, whose no-nonsense approach included promising to shoot any creditor who attempted to seize the monument. He sailed out of Alexandria on June 12, 1880, arriving in Staten Island on July 20 to offload his 220-ton cargo and its 50-ton base onto barges.

Visitors were allowed to visit the obelisk in the hold, although it was covered in wood sheathing (a detail conveniently omitted by some magazine artists), and The World said visitors emerged in "a wild state of enthusiasm."

Martina D'Alton wrote an extensive article on the obelisk in the spring 1993 issue of the Bulletin of the Metropolitan Museum of Art; from the moment it arrived, she said, it was the "best show in town." There were paper models of the obelisk, "Cleopatra dates" and a new drink, the Obbylish. Corticelli Silk Mills issued a trade card with half a dozen putti raising an obelisk with thread.

SPECIAL NOTE: Revelation 11: (8) records that God's Two Candlestick Witnesses shall be killed in the city that is spiritually called Sodom, and Egypt, that it is also the city where our Lord was crucified, meaning Jerusalem. All three of these cities are located in the State of New York.

These are literally the cities of Sodom, Egypt, and Jerusalem.

Chapter 6

Certifying the Rod of God on Washington's Masonic Apron

Cleopatra's Needles, which stood side by side before Pharaoh's house as twins and the number 11, is the rod that God has given Prophet Ellis. A rod measures 11 cubits. This rod is found in the 11th chapter of Revelation and the 11th chapter of Isaiah. It is the symbolism of the two elevens that comprises what has become known in social media as the hashtag. The hashtag is a heraldry emblem made by crossing two elevens representing the 11th chapters of Isaiah and Revelation among other things. Prophet Ellis has shown and proven the hashtag to be a heraldry emblem of Masonry that is used to communicate secret messages in a shorthand language. It takes its name from the House of Hashim. Hashim is the family name for the prophet Muhammad.

The hashtag arrived in America on the George Washington Masonic apron in 1784. The satin apron came as a satirical gift from Paris. It was presented to Washington by Marquis de Lafayette who embroidered on it the hashtag and other Masonic emblems. Marquis de Lafayette was the wife of French general Lafayette who allied with Washington in the war against the British. The apron has among other things on it images of the two witnesses, two candlesticks, the future temple, the seven stars for the seven angels, Jacob's ladder at Bethel, and the triple tau crosses of the crucifixion. The triple tau crosses are hidden behind the hashtag symbolism. The apron was made from the crucifixion apron which Jesus wore on the cross to cover the privacy of his body. The French has the other part including the so-called Shroud of Turin, the burial cloth of Jesus.

This apron is the second centerpiece which appears in all Masonic Bibles with the Washington Memorial. The apron is now in possession of the Grand Lodge of Pennsylvania. It is illustrated in this section 6.

In addition to the Freemasons implying in their own publication, their responsibility to rebuild the Lord's temple, which they now object, the Washington Masonic apron also delivers that obligation by symbolism. It was God's power and favoritism that gave Washington's army victory over the British in 1781 at Yorktown. America has admitted to that favoritism by crafting it on the US Great Seal fixed on the US one dollar treasury note. It is written in the Latin tongue as *annuit coeptis*. It means God has smiled on and favored our undertaking. America had just defeated the most powerful nation in the world to gain its independence. It would now become and remain the most powerful nation in the world. It is for this reason the Lord has compelled them to rebuild His temple.

Prophet Ellis has found via his biblical research that this obligation to build the Lord a house in this great land is not unprecedented. When God gave Cyrus, king of Persia (Iran), all the kingdoms of the earth, He charged Cyrus to build him a house at Jerusalem. "The Lord changes not." He has charged the United States and its G7/G8 to do likewise. However, they do not like his messenger.

The Washington and Lafayette Medallion
From the Original by the Marchioness De Brienne, 1788

The Washington Masonic Apron

In the latter part of 1784 General La Fayette came upon a visit to see Washington, and brought with him a beautiful white satin Masonic apron, upon which the Masonic emblems were beautifully worked by Marquise La Fayette, it being her gift; while the general tendered a beautiful rosewood box.

This apron is now in possession of the Grand Lodge of Pennsylvania

Now in the first year of Cyrus king of Persia, that the word of the Lord by the mouth of Jeremiah might be fulfilled, the Lord stirred up the spirit of Cyrus king of Persia, that he made a proclamation throughout all his kingdom, and put it also in writing, saying, Thus saith Cyrus king of Persia, The Lord God of heaven hath given me all the kingdoms of the earth; and he hath charged me to build him an house at Jerusalem, which is in Judah. Who is there among you of all his people? his God be with him, and let him go up to Jerusalem, which is in Judah, and build the house of the Lord God of Israel, (he is the God,) which is in Jerusalem. And whosoever remaineth in any place where he sojourneth, let the men of his place help him with silver, and with gold, and with goods, and with beasts, beside the freewill offering for the house of God that is in Jerusalem.

And all they that were about them strengthened their hands with vessels of silver, with gold, with goods, and with beasts, and with precious things, beside all that was willingly offered. Also Cyrus the king brought forth the vessels of the house of the Lord, which Nebuchadnezzar had brought forth out of Jerusalem, and had put them in the house of his gods; Even those did Cyrus king of Persia bring forth by the hand of Mithredath the treasurer, and numbered them unto Sheshbazzar, the prince of Judah. (Ezra 1:1–4, 6–8)

Prophet Ellis has broken the codes of the hashtag by the powers and gifts given to him by God through the Holy Spirit. The breaking of these codes shows that the hashtag, as a social media icon, was developed for Freemasons and adopted by the public out of ignorance and the lack of knowledge. God has spoken by the prophet Hosea, saying, "My people are destroyed for lack of knowledge: because thou has rejected knowledge" (Hosea 4:6). Today, Hosea's prophesy on the lack of knowledge is being fulfilled. The hashtag is unto America as the Pied Piper was to the children of Hamelin. The hashtag is destroying both the rats and the children who lack knowledge concerning this ambitious shorthand emblem.

The hashtag is a Masonic emblem showing how the garment of Jesus was divided among the soldiers who crucified him.

> Then the soldiers, when they had crucified Jesus, took his garments, and made four parts, to every soldier a part; and also his coat: now the coat was without seam, woven from the top throughout. (John 19:23)

Notes

REFERENCES: Masonic Bibles Questions and Answers (p.23)

Question: Who presented Washington with an embroidered satin apron?

Answer: Madame La Fayette—The apron was conveyed by the Marquis from Paris to General Washington at Mt. Vernon. It is preserved by the Washington Benevolent Society at Philadelphia, and the Grand Lodge of Pennsylvania. It is the most prized relic of Masonry in the USA.

Question: Masonically, what may be said of the Boston Tea Party?

Answer: It had its installation in a Masonic Lodge Room; all participating in the raid, were Masons.

Question: What noted Patriot, killed in the battle of Bunker Hill, was a Mason?

Answer: General Warren.

Question: How many signers of the Declaration of Independence were Masons?

Answer: Fifty-three.

Question: Was Masonry practiced in the Revolutionary War?

Answer: Yes.

Question: Who was the first Master of Alexandria Lodge No. 22, Alexandria, Virginia?

Answer: George Washington

Question: Where was Washington initiated?

Answer: Fredericksburg, Virginia, A.D. 1752

Question: Did Washington follow the Masonic custom when he laid the cornerstone of the new Capitol building in 1739?

Answer: No. It was laid in the Southeast corner.

Question: Name five of the ten early Presidents of the United States who were Masons?

Answer: Washington, Monroe, Jackson, Polk and Buchanan.

Question: Anti-Masonic excitement: In what states were its effects most felt?

Answer: New England, especially New York and Pennsylvania.

Question: When did it occur in the United States?

Answer: 1826

Question: What caused it?

Answer: The disappearances and alleged abduction of one William Morgan.

Question: Was he a Mason?

Answer: Claimed to have been made a Mason in Canada, or some foreign country.

Question: Koran: What is it?

Answer: The sacred book of the Mohammedans. In a Lodge consisting wholly of Mohammedans, it would be esteemed as the book of the Law, and take the place on the altar occupied in Christian Lodges by the Bible.

Chapter 7

Key of David Unwrap Twitter's Hashtag Heraldry and Twitter Closes Thousands of ISIS Accounts

The voluminous and sophisticated prophetic library of Prophet Ellis shows that Twitter is one of thousands of secret Masonic corporations. His library also includes certified court documents from Cause Number C-06-006-72-VRW in the US district court, Western District of California, at San Francisco. It is a cause that Ellis requested the Court to consolidate with his cause filed against the Freemasons under Cause Number A05-CA-682-LY in the Western District of Texas at Austin. In these, Ellis sought the return of Solomon's treasure and an order to force the Freemasons to rebuild the house of God. That battle still continues today.

In his petition, Prophet Ellis broke many ancient Freemasonry codes including the secret rod of God hidden on the Washington apron, one published and sealed under the terms of heraldry. His open revelations into the public records of the courts forced the Freemasons hand to disseminate a global bulletin to a secret audience of ranking masons. The hashtag would be that smart and ambitious emblem that could speak a thousand words in a Masonic shorthand language. Just a few months later and a few blocks over from where the courthouse stood, Twitter was born. Its hashtag and its Twitter bird would tweet a message that would be just as complicated as one trying to decipher Tuvan throat singing. In a *New York Times*'s article dated November 4, 2012, its reporter Julia Turner called the hashtag the Tuvan throat singer of today's Internet.

Ellis records confirm that only ranking masons are taught the true hashtag language behind the steel doors and soundproof walls of its Masonic Lodges. The hashtag would announce that God has sent forth the promised and prophetic rod out of the Stem of Jesse. This rod would guarantee a new kind of US president in 2008. It has all come to pass.

Prophet Ellis became frustrated and disgusted that US law enforcement was unwilling to shut down ISIS Twitter accounts that were being used to solicit western fighters and promote their cause for a holy war on Christians. The beheading of Christians was being shown daily. To a novice in both logic and law enforcement, it was obvious to Prophet Ellis that some wicked power had given ISIS a green invisible light while US law enforcement looked the other way. Prophet Ellis quickly realized that if Twitter is Masonry and Masonry is Satan, that this would make Twitter exempt from prosecution by American law enforcement. In other words, they get off "Scott Free." Scott Free is that part of a dark sentence alluding to immunity from prosecution granted to Scottish Rite Freemasons under terms of their covenant with the order.

A covenant is a contract or agreement between two or more parties on certain terms. In becoming a mason, a man enters into a covenant with the fraternity, agreeing to fulfill certain promises and perform certain duties. On the other hand, the fraternity and its members bind themselves to certain ties of friendship, brotherliness, protection, support, and benefits. The breaking of a covenant is subject to stated penalties; the Masonic covenant includes specific and deadly penalties.

On January 17, 2015, Ellis, while using the rod that God placed in his mouth (Isa. 11:4), unwrapped Twitter's hashtag heraldry in a revealing press release. On February 20, 2015, just one month later, the US Congress asked Twitter if it would close ISIS accounts. It had no authority to demand such. Twitter agreed because it had been exposed. I am only able to articulate this historical event by including the actual graphics from Prophet Ellis's press release in this portion of my thesis.

TERMS OF HERALDRY

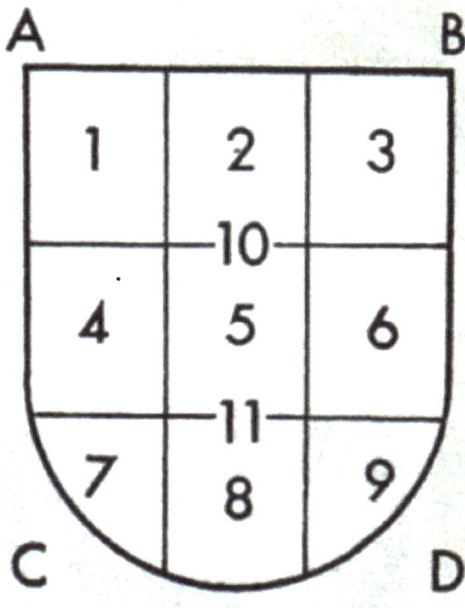

8 Base point
9 Sinister canton of base
10 Honour point
11 Nombril point
A-B Upper margin
C-D Lower margin
A-C Dexter margin
B-D Sinister margin
1-2-3 Chief
4-5-6 Fesse
7-8-9 Base
1-4-7 Dexter tierce
2-5-8 Pale
3-6-9 Sinister tierce

1 Dexter chief canton
2 Chief point
3 Sinister chief canton
4 Dexter flank
5 Center point
6 Sinister flank
7 Dexter canton of base

WREATH OR BANDEAU

It is composed of six twists, either curved or straight, and has the same tinctures as shield and charges, the metal in all cases being the first twist on the dexter side.

CANDLESTICK MINISTRIES

AN OPEN MESSAGE TO MANY

Prophet W. H. "Bill" Ellis
Published January 17, 2015

TWITTERS' SECRET HASHTAG HERALDRY UNWRAPPED

The Epicenter of Terror Exposed!!

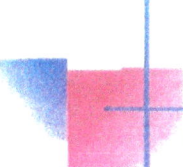

PROPHET W. H. "BILL" ELLIS

January 17, 2015

SUBJECT: BROKEN CODES OF THE HASHTAG AND ITS TWITTER
BIRD REVEALS A SECRET CORPORATE TERROR EMPIRE

This letter is opened to the general public online. It has been sent to multiple parties both inside, and outside of governments in order to prevent inactions and/or cover-ups. This strategy was warranted because I have identified those who are using their public office to shield TWITTER and others form their secret alliance with ISIS, and other Terror groups. They are united by what they have defined as the Mystic Tie. Broken heraldry codes for the hashtag has revealed that Mystic Tie which is scientifically illustrated in my enclosed documents which are also posted online.

COPIES OF THIS MESSAGE SENT TO:
ERIC HOLDER AND/OR LORETTA LYNCH, U.S. ATTY. GEN.
TWITTER, INC. CORPORATE HEADQUARTERS
WILLIAM BRATTON, N.Y.C. POLICE COMMISSIONER
PATRICK LYNCH, PBA PRESIDENT
CHARLES RAMSEY, PHILADELPHIA POLICE COMMISSIONER
REV. AL SHARPTON, HOUSE OF JUSITCE
REV. JESSE JACKSON, RAINBOW/PUSH
BENJAMIN CRUMP, ATTORNEY
AND OTHERS.

The hashtag is a public name for the heraldry term hash mark. It is a verb, and a secret ancient Arabic Order from the House of Hashem. It carries a hidden directive to mark, label, or tag a person or property to be wiped out, and/or destroyed. Paris presented the hashtag to America in 1784 as a satirical gift. It was embroidered on part of Jesus' crucifixion apron that was made into a Masonic apron for President George Washington. The TWITTTER blue legless Martlet signals that the Mystic-Tie is a spiritual bond which cannot be traced by finger, and footprints.

The Martlet is the mark of the fourth son of cadency, and it occupies lot four on the hashtag under Terms of Heraldry. The Islamic crescent is the second, and its five-pointed star is the third. They occupy lot 2, and lot 3 on the hashtag. Paris' Fleur-de-lis is the sixth mark. It was the emblem of King Charles VII, aka Charlie Hedbo. Hedbo means seven. It occupies lot six on the hashtag. Hashem is the family name of the prophet Muhammad which inspired the TWITTER term hashtag. It is a sophisticated and diverse heraldic, and spiritual messenger. It gave the illusive instructions for the execution of the two New York city Police Officers, and also the Terror attacks in Paris. It is currently being used to tag others. It is a diabolical strategy used to create confusion and chaos, and to foil peaceful and prophetic movements for justice and reforms. This foil is the ninth mark that is called the octofoil. TWITTER termed it the octothrope. It is veiled as the 9th, but is actually the 8th because the first is rejected. The first is Christ from who the hashtag originated as a sacred crucifixion garment.

Prophet W. H. "Bill" Ellis

Notes

REFERENCES: www.quora.com…Government

Why can't the U. S. Government close the ISIS Twitter account….Has the U. S. Government pressured Twitter to take down ISIS's account?

TWO ANSWERS: 9 want answers. 2,180 views.

Carter Moore, Political Science, BA, (His Answer) Because the US government doesn't own Twitter. They would have to either lean on Twitter, Inc., to do it themselves, or get a court to force Twitter, a US-owned company, to shut down the accounts of non-US citizens that may or may not violate either free speech laws or Twitter's own terms of service. (Written September 2, 2014).

Nick Malik (Business Strategists, Enterprise Archite…

Twitter doesn't charge money for their services. Therefore US trade law is unclear about whether the company has to cut ties. The way the law is written, the government has to provide the name of a person that cannot transact with an American company on the "denied parties list". But Twitter doesn't require a name. Or a transaction. So how is that enforced?

If they want to close that particular account, they could get a court order, but what would stop ISIS from opening a new one? So let's say a congressman introduces a bill to outlaw free services from being provided to denied parties. It would be strongly opposed by Google, Facebook, Microsoft, Twitter, and dozens of internet companies. Their might along would get the bill squashed.

We believe in free speech. If we can handle Nazi, a few Islamic militants are no big deal. (written Sept. 5, 2014)

Worldnews.com (February 18, 2015) Congress asks Twitter to shut down ISIS Accounts: Congress is putting pressure on social media sites to shut down accounts used by terror groups.

Congress members ask FBI to shut down Hamas Twitter account: Seven House Republicans have called for Twitter to take down the accounts of "US-designated terror groups." Led by Texas Congressman Ted Poe (R-Tex), the lawmakers…

Twitter Escalates Its Own ISIS Battle: 2000 Accounts Suspended Last Week. ABC News March 2, 2015.

Anonymous: Hacking Group Reportedly Shut Down Hundreds of Social Media Accounts Ties to ISIS. (The Inquister: March 12, 2015)

Chapter 8

The Code Name "Hashtag" Broken and Analyzed and Validated the Key of David

The hashtag as used by Twitter is a form of heraldry belonging to a particular family. It belongs to the House of Hashim. This is the family name of the prophet Muhammad who is the founder of Islam. The American College of Heraldry and the British College of Heraldry are good sources to acquire information regarding the origin, use, and purpose of heraldry both as an art and a science. The American College of Heraldry is a chartered, nonprofit body established in 1972. According to its website home page, its aim is aiding in the study and perpetuation of heraldry in the United States and abroad.

In their "Introduction," they write, "Heraldry is at once an art and a science. Its origins are rooted in the social and political structure which existed in Europe and the British isles from about the year 1100 AD. However, far from being an obsolete relic of a bygone era, heraldry has rather emerged as a vibrant and growing cultural form. Legitimate coats of arms are more widely used throughout the world today than ever before in history."

The College continue, saying, "While Americans are usually fascinated by the beauty of heraldry, they are rarely familiar with its meaning and traditions and, therefore, often misunderstand and even abuse this rich cultural heritage. They seldom understand that a coat of arms is usually granted, certified, registered, or otherwise recognized as belonging to one individual alone and that only his direct descendants with proven linage can be recognized as eligible to inherit the arms. Exceptions to this rule are rare." Enters the hashtag name for the House of Hashim. However odd, it is rightfully called the hashtag.

As Prophet Ellis has illustrated using the hashtag shown under "Terms of Heraldry," the nine sons of cadency each occupy one of the nine sections on the hashtag. Islam's crescent and five-pointed star occupies lot 2 and lot 3. Twitter's legless Martin, which is called a Marlet, occupies lot 4. The legless bird conveys by symbolism that he leaves no finger or footprints that would allow one to track him. This legless bird is the heraldry emblem of several large American companies including Marten Transport. American Express uses it on one of its money cards with a cunning slogan alluding to its hidden feet. Their card carries a slogan that says, "Many Features, No Fees," meaning "many feathers, no feet." These are just a few of the many dark sentences that Prophet Ellis has broken by using an ancient and golden key, which is called the Key of David.

The unveiled Twitter bird unveils the world's largest scandal working in concert with terrorists. There is a mystic tie that connects the western Freemasonry brotherhood to the Muslim brotherhood. Their link, Prophet Ellis has shown and I have confirmed, is hidden under layers of tricky veils, dark sentences, and code words and symbols that are indefinable because of their spiritual nature that was sealed. God himself has unsealed them so that they may become exposed in these troubled times.

The rose under the terms of heraldry is the mark of the seventh son of cadency. It belongs to the Yorkists and Lancasters of the Grand Lodge of England. These are the families that once warred against each other in what became known as War of the Roses. The three are united and tied together by their numerical place values under terms of heraldry as 237.

Notes

REFERENCES: Internetslang.com

HASHTAG DEFINITION: The definition of Hashtag is "Label on Twitter to aid searching."

So now you know *hashtag* means "label on Twitter to aid searching," don't thank us. YM!

NOTE: The foregoing answer although cunning, did come from an authority. Under the "Terms of Heraldry", "Label" is the mark of the first Son of Cadency. It alludes to Jesus and the malefactors who were crucified along with him. (Refer to Terms of Heraldry in the previous chapter).

REFERENCES: Nicklewiscommunications.com: What does A # Hashtag/Pound Sign Actually Mean in Social Media? Posted by Nick Lewis on March 21, 2013 in Blog. Hashtags, Social Media. Twitter.

The pound sign or hashtag is visually represented by the symbol "#", and by placing the symbol in front of a word (or series of words) on a social network, it will turn that word into a metadata tag. In simple English, the # symbol turns the word(s) immediately following it into a searchable term that can be used on that website or social network, which is activated by someone clicking on that hashtag.

Chapter 9

The Code Name Pound Sign Broken and Analyzed and Validated the Key of David

Although it is classified and kept from the ears of most citizens, the return of Jesus Christ to reign over the earth is at the forefront of business for all nations. The kings and princes of the earth have long been corrupted by money and material wealth. Therefore, Jesus spoke a parable concerning his going away and returning to reign as King, which has troubled the nations for many centuries. The parable spoken by Jesus in the 19th chapter of Luke's gospel inspired what has become known as the pound sign. It is the name of the currency used by the British and several other countries. Jesus would give ten pounds to ten servants and tell them to "Occupy till he come." Occupy is an ancient term for trading. This parable inspired the movement, which became internationally known as Occupy Wall Street.

> And as they heard these things, he added and spake a parable, because he was nigh to Jerusalem, and because they thought that the kingdom of God should immediately appear. He said therefore, A certain nobleman went into a far country to receive for himself a kingdom, and to return. And he called his ten servants, and delivered them ten pounds, and said unto them, Occupy till I come.
>
> But his citizens hated him, and sent a message after him, saying, We will not have this man to reign over us. And it came to pass, that when he was returned, having received the kingdom, then he commanded these servants to be called unto him, to whom he had given the money, that he might know how much every man had gained by trading.
>
> Then came the first, saying, Lord, thy pound hath gained ten pounds. And he said unto him, Well, thou good servant: because thou hast been faithful in a very little, have thou authority over ten cities.
>
> And the second came, saying, Lord, thy pound hath gained five pounds. And he said likewise to him, Be thou also over five cities. And another came, saying, Lord, behold, here is thy pound, which I have kept laid up in a napkin: For I feared thee, because thou art an austere man: thou takest up that thou layedst not down, and reapest that thou didst not sow.
>
> And he saith unto him, Out of thine own mouth will I judge thee, thou wicked servant. Thou knewest that I was an austere man, taking up that I laid not down, and reaping that I did not sow: Wherefore then gavest not thou my money into the bank, that at my coming I might have required mine own with usury?
>
> And he said unto them that stood by, Take from him the pound, and give it to him that hath ten pounds. (And they said unto him, Lord, he hath ten pounds.) For I say unto you, That unto every one which hath shall be given; and from him that hath not, even that he hath shall be taken away from him. But those mine enemies, which would not that I should reign over them, bring hither, and slay them before me. (Luke 19:11–27)

This parable of the one pound, being given unto the servant having ten pounds, thus making a total of eleven pounds, is hidden on the pound sign emblem under terms of heraldry. The hashtag or pound sign is numbered to eleven although there are only nine lots. (See terms of heraldry.)

The symbol that is used for pound (lb.) alludes to the scientific term for this emblem which is called label. It seems that the practical symbol for pound would be *pd*. This broken code used for pound ties the pound sign directly to the scientific heraldry and the crucifixion of Jesus. This door could not have been opened without the Key of David.

Notes

REFERENCES: Languagelog.idc.upen.edu

The "pound sign mystery" July 18, 2010: Filed by Mark Liberman under words-words-words-

Yesterday, in discussing Kevin Fowler's song Pound Sign, there was some debate about the origin of the term "pound sign" for the symbol #. I suggested that it all started with the substitution of # for the symbol £ on American typewriter keyboards, but others argued that # was a standard symbol for pound(s) avoirdupois. I've heard this theory before, but I expressed skepticism about it because I've never actually seen the symbol used that way.

Today, after some further research, I'm still not completely sure. But I've found a new theory, which I think has a better chance to be correct: It's all Emile Baudot's fault.

William Safire asked about this usage in his On Language column for 1/20/1991, "MAIL CALL (ALL CAPS)":

...you and I rarely use suite or even apartment number, abbreviated to Apt. No.; most often, we use the crosshatch symbol for "number", which has come to be known as the pound sign (origin and etymology of which I seek Lex Irreg help in finding).

Others writing about the same time indicate that this usage was unfamiliar to them as well. Thus Ron Alexander, "Metropolitan Diary", NYT 6/20/1990:

The responses are delivered in a reassuring, synthesized male voice that never hesitates or sneezes or coughs. It says to "push the pound sign after entering the deposit amount". The pound sign, the voice explains, "is to the right of the zero: the asterisk is to the left of the zero.

I believe that AT&T used "pound sign" for this symbol from the first introduction of the touchtone keypad in 1963, but it's clear that in 1990-1991 the term was still new to many Americans. I left AT&T in 1990, and at that point, "touch-tone penetration" (as we used to call it) was still low enough to be an argument for outfitting voice response systems with speech recognition technology, even though that technology was then very expensive and not very robust.

NOTE: The pound sign remained a mystery to the foregoing writer.

Chapter 10

The Number and Tic-Tac-Toe Code
Broken and Analyzed and Validated the Key of David

The hashtag is used to play a children's game known as tic-tac-toe. The object of the game is to line three crosses (XXX) in a row, as the three were lined for the crucifixion. The *X* is the 22nd Greek alphabet called "chi" and is traditionally used to represent Christ, who was martyred on the cross.

Tic is the fatigue or convulsive reaction of the muscles causing them to twitch and jerk. When Jesus's muscles would begin to tic, after many hours of suffering, the Roman soldiers would tac his toe. It became a game for those who chose to mock the crucifixion of our Savior. Under the terms of heraldry for the mark of the first son, this mark is inverted to keep it from being discerned. Prophet Ellis, by the power of the Holy Spirit and the Key of David, has opened the doors that has kept the dark secrets of the nations hidden for many centuries.

This cross is the 22nd Hebrew alphabet which is called "taw." When the three are placed together, it is called 322, which is a code used by Freemasonry alluding to the skull and bones of Jesus. Skull and Bones is a secret society of Freemasonry that was organized by Islamic nobles to undermine the resurrection of Jesus. The opponents would do this by using skulls and bones from an ancient tomb and present these publicly as being the skull and bones of Jesus, his wife Mary Magdalene, and their son Judah. The scheme was the subject of a February 2007 Discovery Channel documentary, produced by Hollywood filmmaker James Cameron and directed by Toronto filmmaker Simcha Jacobovici. Prophet Ellis foiled the scheme when he broke and disclosed the ancient mysteries of Skull and Bones. The documentary disappeared under a veil of silence and shame. Their hope was to disprove the resurrection by alleging his bones are still in his tomb.

News organizations around the world along with those who have for centuries taught their followers that there was no resurrection, were rejoicing at what many called a historic revelation. They were unaware that God had positioned a messenger in the earth who would quickly expose their hoax of these skulls and bones, which did not belong to Jesus.

The hashtag or number sign is positioned above the number 3 on all computer keyboards to signal the three crucified and code 322. Twenty-two (22) is the sum of the two elevens forming the hashtag. This code also alludes to the 2.2 pounds which equals to one kilogram. Thirdly, 322 encrypts the mark of the second son of Cadency with the mark of the third son. When combined, they form the chief emblem of Islam the crescent and star. The crescent and star are also the emblems of Masonry's Shriners, which alludes to this Mystic Shrine that is alleged to be that of Jesus and wife Mary Magdalene and their alleged son Judah.

According to Freemasonry documents archived in Prophet Ellis's prophetic library, the Shriners were organized in Mecca, Saudi Arabia, in 644 AD shortly after the death of the prophet Muhammad. The scheme, which has now been foiled, entailed using the skull and bones of another person and then putting them in a shrine labeled as the shrine of Jesus. They would pretend that the shrine was discovered by chance in 1980 by construction workers. It was a diabolical spiritual undertaking that leaves no visible footprints. This is the symbolism put forth by the Twitter feetless Martin. They could only be exposed by God through his messenger unto the nations. The Shriners are at the summit of Masonry. One must have the rank of a 32-degree Mason before he becomes eligible for membership. Their aim and purpose are hidden from most ranking members.

Skeptics target new Jesus film

The Lost Tomb implies he wed Mary Magdalene and fathered a son

By DION NISSENBAUM
MCCLATCHY-TRIBUNE

JERUSALEM — The Academy Award-winning director behind *Titanic* and *The Terminator* is attempting to challenge fundamental tenets of Christianity by suggesting that Jesus may have been a father whose body was buried far from the Jerusalem tomb where believers say he rose from the dead.

In a documentary set to air Sunday, Hollywood filmmaker James Cameron and his team contend that they've produced new evidence that Jesus married Mary Magdalene and fathered a son named Judah.

Biblical experts and archaeologists who are familiar with the central evidence instantly discounted the claim, which the Discovery Channel has touted as possibly "the greatest archaeological find in history," as an ill-informed, recycled publicity grab.

Contradicts beliefs

The chances that the findings in *The Lost Tomb of Jesus* are real "are more than remote," Israel Museum curator David Mevorah said. "They are closer to fantasy."

If proved true, the findings would undercut Christian beliefs that Jesus never had children and that he rose from the dead. The documentary also contradicts long-held beliefs by Roman Catholic and Orthodox Christians that Jesus had lain in a tomb around which Christians built the Church of the Holy Sepulcher in the Old City of Jerusalem.

"It doesn't get bigger than this," Cameron said before the basic findings were presented Monday at a New York news conference. "We've done our homework; we've made the case, and now it's time for the debate to begin."

Simcha Jacobovici, the Toronto filmmaker who directed the documentary, said the implications "are huge."

"But they're not necessarily the implications people think they are. For example, some believers are going to say, well this challenges the resurrection. I don't know why, if Jesus rose from one tomb, he couldn't have risen from the other tomb," Jacobovici told *Today*.

2,000-year-old tomb

The Discovery Channel documentary and an accompanying book center on a 2,000-year-old limestone tomb that was discovered more than a quarter-century ago during a construction project in a residential Jerusalem neighborhood between the Old City and Bethlehem.

When the tomb was uncovered in 1980, specialists were called. The man who led the effort was Amos Kloner, an archaeologist from Bar Ilan University, who meticulously documented the findings.

The tomb contained 10 limestone burial boxes and scattered bones. Among the inscriptions on the ancient caskets: Jesus, son of Joseph; Mary; and Judah, son of Jesus.

Five of the burial boxes, known as ossuaries, had names that could be linked to the Bible, including versions of Joseph and Matthew.

Then and now, Kloner took no note of the names, saying they were common among area residents at the time.

Skeptical scholar

Stephen Pfann, a biblical scholar at the University of the Holy Land in Jerusalem who was interviewed in the documentary, said the film's hypothesis holds little weight.

"I don't think that Christians are going to buy into this," Pfann said. "But skeptics, in general, would like to see something that pokes holes into the story that so many people hold dear."

"How possible is it?" Pfann said. "On a scale of one through 10 — 10 being completely possible — it's probably a one, maybe a one and a half."

The Associated Press contributed to this report.

MYSTERY DEEPENS: Jacobovici says 10 ossuaries found in this cave in 1980 may have held bones of Jesus, his wife Mary Magdalene and possibly their son Judah.

The Shriners were organized with the official name "Ancient Arabic Order of Nobles of the Mystic Shrine." After Prophet Ellis exposed their scheme of this shrine and their connection to radical Islam, they, thereafter, quietly changed their official name. Today, their new official name is "Shriners International." Among them are men of power and wealth.

Why is the hashtag also called the number sign? None of the codes for the hashtag that were broken by Prophet Ellis are disconnected from the crucifixion. The hashtag is called a number sign based on a prophesy by Jeremiah, which foretold the Lord being numbered along with two other malefactors. For the best understanding, one must remember that the hashtag that is divided into nine sections illustrates how Jesus garments were divided among the soldiers who crucified him. That pattern has been adopted as the head ornament worn on the headgear of US Servicemen. The gospel of Mark encodes the skull and bones, the divided garment among the soldiers, and the number sign all in a few verses. Mark writes as follows:

And they compel one Simon a Cyrenian, who passed by, coming out of the country, the father of Alexander and Rufus, to bear his cross. And they bring him unto the place Golgotha, which is, being interpreted, The place of a skull. [Give special attention to Golgotha.] And they gave him to drink wine mingled with myrrh: but he received it not. And when they had crucified him, they parted his garments, casting lots upon them, what every man should take.

And it was the third hour, and they crucified him. And the superscription of his accusation was written over, THE KING OF THE JEWS. And with him they crucify two thieves; the one on his right hand, and the other on his left. And the scripture was fulfilled, which saith, And he was numbered with the transgressors. (Mark 15:21–28)

Prophet Ellis's illustrations were so profound, original, and biblically rooted, that it was absolutely clear to me that God had chosen him for special messianic work among the nations. These could not have been accomplished without him possessing the golden Key of David.

The hashtag, as it appears under the terms of heraldry, is worn as a head ornament by US Servicemen. Many of those who are charged with the day-to-day policies and operations of US Arm Forces are not Christians. They are honored to use complex symbolism to mock a religion, which they do not believe in. This head ornament is worn in the movie titled *Shoot the Messenger*, alluding to what will happen to God's two witnesses who will expose the hidden evils among the nations (Rev. 11:7–14).

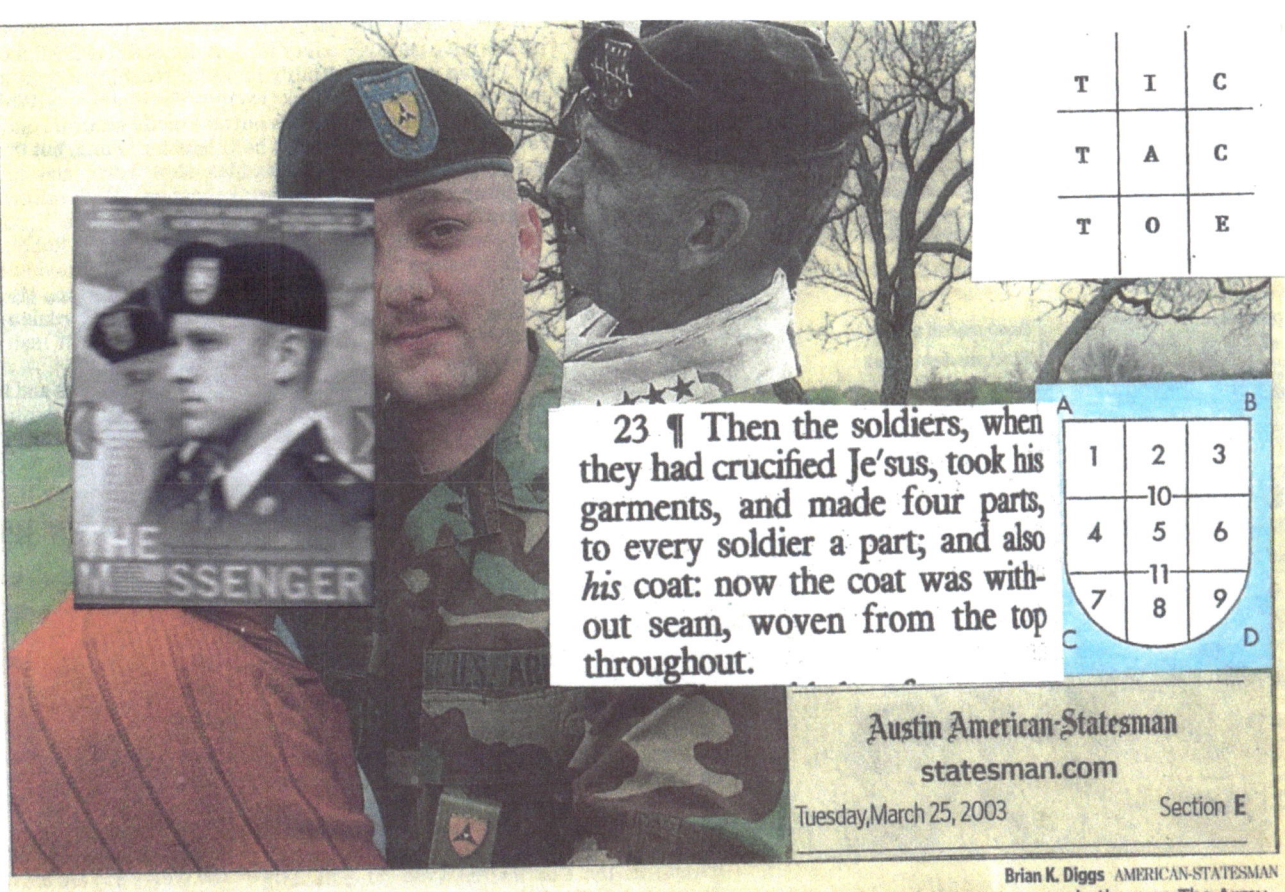

Chris Cox studies criminal justice at Austin Community College, but he's putting school on the back burner to serve in the war. The Army reservist is now at Fort Hood, waiting to head to the Middle East. His wife, Kristin, visited him several times at the base last week.

Notes

REFERENCES: Blog.dictionary.com What is the Real Name of the #? 6/25/2012:

On Facebook and Twitter, you tag your friends with the @ symbol and topics with the #. If you see something that says #wordoftheday, the tweet or post will concern the Word of the Day in some way. But what do you call the # symbol? Where did it come from? Its myriad names and its appearance are intertwined.

The # symbol is commonly called the pound sign, number sign and more recently the hashtag. It is called the pound sign because the symbol comes from the abbreviation for weight, lb. or "libra pondo" literally pound by weight" in LATIN. When writing lb. it was not uncommon for scribes to cross the letters across the top with a line across the top. like a t.

The phrase "number sign" arose in Britain because "pound sign" could easily be confused with the British currency. The # symbol is sometimes spoken as the word "number", as in the word "number two pencil". But what is the official name? The octothrope. (Note: This name octo comes from the Mark of the eight Son of Cadency: See Terms of Heraldry)

What does that mean? It is actually a made up word. It was invented in the same laboratories where the telephone came from. The scientists at Bell Laboratories modified the telephone keypad in the early 1960s and added the # symbol to send instructions to the telephone operating system. Since the # symbol didn't have a name, the technicians made one up. They knew it should be called "octo"—something because it has eight ends around the edge. But how to make "octo" into a noun? What happened next is not entirely clear. According to one report, Bell lab employee Don MacPherson named it after the Olympian Jim Thorpe. Another former employee claims it was a nonsense word that is a joke. Another unverifiable report is much more etymologically satisfying. The Old Norse word "thrope" meant "farm or field", so octothrope literally means "eight fields." (Note: Field is a heraldry term referring to the ground of each division of a shield or flag.)

The word hash predates these other terms but was not very popular unit recently. (Maybe because it reminds us of mediocre diner food.) It first referred to stripes on military jackets as early as 1910. In the 1980's, it came to refer to the # symbol. Since the ascent of social media, hashtag has become the favored word for the # symbol.

NOTE: There is a common thread which connects all these questions and answers. That common thread is the myriad names of the hashtag which are all interwoven, making a puzzle like fitting to the crucifixion garment of Jesus. This garment that was soaked in blood is a sign of his imminent return. (Revelation 19:11-16)

Chapter 11

The Hashtag's Y2K Code Broken and Analyzed and Validated the Key of David

This section 11 requires the use of graphics for illustrating how the code Y2K was used as a code for the hashtag and 9/11 for use in public domain without detection. As the year 2000 approached, many people thought that Y2K was Roman numerals for year 2000. However, Y2K is just another Freemasonry code used for 9/11 and the hashtag. The hashtag has nine sections created by two sets of elevens. One 11 is vertical, and the other is horizontal, thus creating nine sections. Nine is the numerical place value for the ninth English alphabet *I*. Therefore, since *Y* and *I* sometimes have interchangeable phonetic sounds, *Y* would be a veil for the number 9.

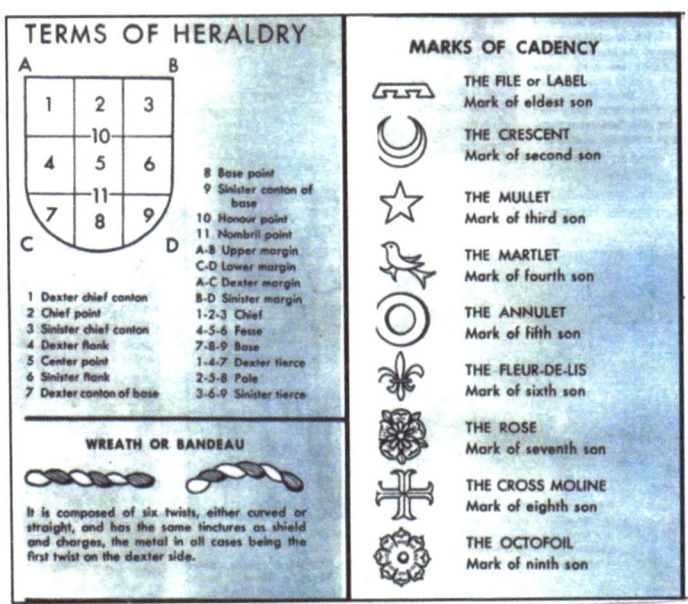

The letter *K* is the eleventh English alphabet. Since there are two elevens that make up the hashtag, it would therefore be 2K. These two codes were thereby combined as Y2K. This was the hidden code for the hashtag and 9/11.

An international secret printing method has been established by the nations to speak covertly about the three crucified and the return of Jesus. It is the language of the International Alphabet Flag Code. Red, yellow, and blue are the colors of the three crosses corresponding to the letters *R*, *V*, and *X*. The color of each cross identifies the character of each of the three men on the cross. Red represents Jesus whose blood was shed for the faithful. The color blue was the malefactor who believed on Jesus and whom Jesus promised would be in paradise with him. Yellow is for the malefactor who was a coward and railed Jesus, saying, "If thou be Christ, save thyself and us" (Luke 23:39–43).

HP, who makes copiers and computers, uses symbolism to signal that one needs more than just a microscope to detect this mystery of the cross. HP depicts this mystery with a white cross on red, yellow, and blue lines.

Separate sources for my endnotes in chapters 9 and 10 claim that the hashtag, as used now by the phone companies, were developed in the laboratories of AT&T and Bell. Prophet Ellis, through his complex analysis, has shown that red, yellow, and blue are codes for 9/11 that were used by AT&T as early as 1994.

The 1994 AT&T 9/11 brochure, which Prophet Ellis collected and complied in his prophetic library for this day, is just one example of hundreds illustrating how he collected data under the guidance of the Holy Spirit. The red, yellow, and blue are complex Freemasonry codes for 9/11. These doors holding these deep secrets can only be opened by the Key of David. The red square with the one-dollar bill with the letter *S* for September and the number 11 drawn therein are not a dollar sign. It is a code for 9/11. A prophet is one who speaks ahead of those things to come later.

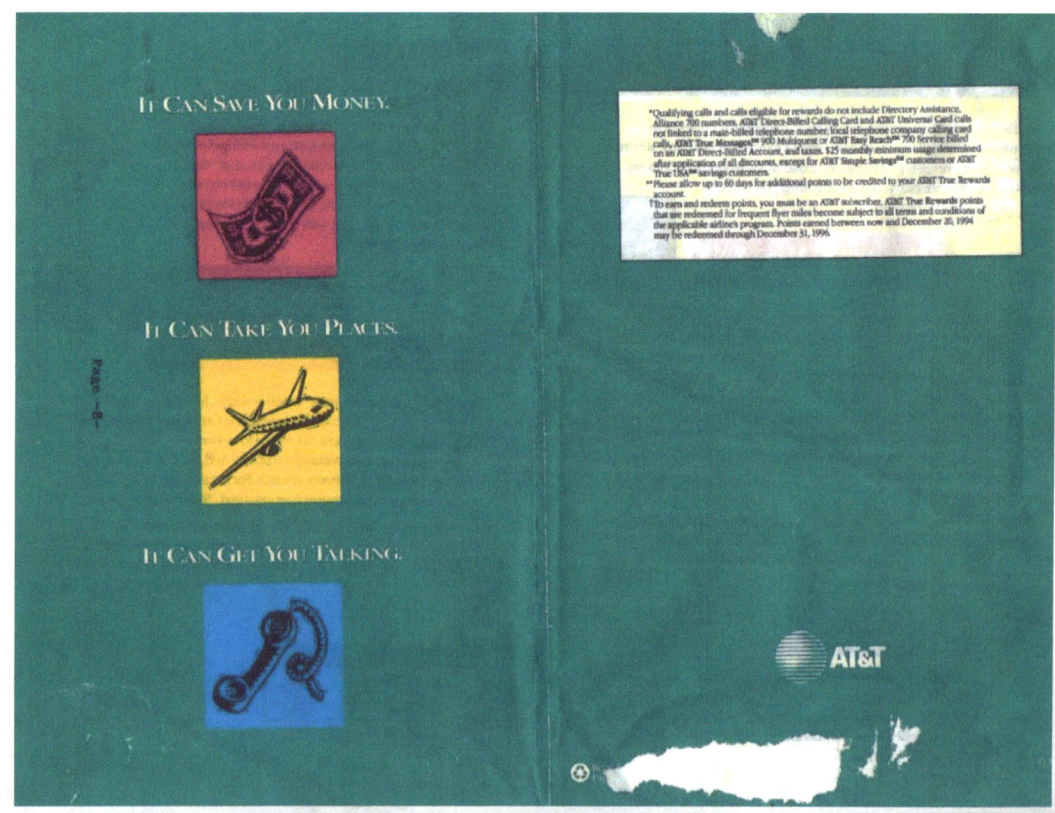

The 33-degree emblem of Freemasonry is a nine-pointed star that embodies the same symbolism as the nine-sectioned hashtag under terms of heraldry. The numbered emblem in this illustration is unique and is created by Prophet Ellis to break the 9/11 code, which also appears on the hashtag. God revealed this mystery to Prophet Ellis instructing him to take the emblem in the center of the two-numbered emblems and enlarge and number each point of the star. He was instructed to number it both clockwise and counterclockwise as shown on the right. This unique pattern revealed a 9/11 mystery connecting the emblem to the hashtag and many other 9/11 unsolved mysteries. Among these is the 9/11 blueprint on my following page, where the hashtag and Masonry's nine-pointed star are symbolic fonts.

When any two numbers on the right emblem above are added, their sum will always equal nine. Here are some examples: 1 + 8 = 9, 2 + 7 = 9, 3 + 6 = 9, and 4 + 5 = 9. On the left, their sum is equal to eleven when the two corresponding numbers are added. Examples are the following: 9 + 2 = 11, 8 + 3 = 11, 7 + 4 = 11, and 6 + 5 = 11. The cross (X), which appears on the back of the emblem with a right hand, symbolizes the hand of one being crucified. This door could not have been opened without this keystone that God has given to Prophet Ellis to do the work of God.

Q 3 3 N Y
✈ 📄 📄 ☠ ✡

A B C D E F G H I J K L
M N O P Q R S T U V X Y
Z

✌ 👌 👍 👎 👉 👈 ☝ 👇 ✋ ☺ 😐 ☹

💣 ☠ ⚑ ⚐ ✈ ☀ 💧 ❄ † ✝ ✠ ✡

☪

1 2 3 4 5 6 7 8 9 0
! @ # $ % ^ & * ( ) _ +

📁 📄 📄 📑 🗔 ⌛ ⌨ 🖱 ☏ 📷

✎ ✃ ✄ ∞ 🔔 ♈ 📖 ✉ ☎ ☏ ♉ ✉

Notes

CHRISTIAN NEWS: Special Issue on Masonry: Vol.31. NO.21. Monday 5/24/1993

Headlines read: "Masonry Is Anti-Christian"

A showdown on Freemasonry's incompatibility with Christianity is coming at next month's Southern Baptist Convention reports the May 17 Christianity Today.

Commenting in a report on the issue by the SBC's Home Mission Board, Dr. James Holly, a Southern Baptist physician, says that "Southern Baptist have become the first Christian denomination that essentially blesses the Masonic Lodge." Christianity Today said that "Holly believes the report is compromised because HMB leaders are fearful of financial fallout. Indeed, of the 3.5 million Masons in the nation, 1.3 million are Southern Baptists, according to Associated Baptist Press. In addition 14 per cent of SBC pastors and 18 percent of deacon board chairs are Masons."

Freemasonry is an anti-Christian religion says the Lutheran Church Missouri Synod (LCMS). The constitution of this church body says that its pastors and laymen are not to join the Masons. The LCMS constitution that the LCMS' has declared itself firmly opposed to all societies, lodges, and organizations of an unchristian or anti-Christian character."

The LCMS declares in a section of its Handbook titled "Fraternal Organizations." Pastors and laymen alike must avoid membership or participation in any organization that in its objectives, ceremonies, or practices is inimical to the Gospel of Jesus Christ of the faith and life or the Christian Church." Most major Protestant denominations allow their pastors and laymen to be Masons.

The LCMS notes that Masonry conducts worship services, has prayers and funeral services and insists masonry is therefore a religion.

Additional Source: Houston Chronicle, Reporter James Giddons:

Article title: "Pastor leads GOP in prayer for sins of "white church". FORT WORTH—A white minister from Jasper County led state Republicans Saturday in a prayer of forgiveness for the sins of the "white church" in response to the brutal killing of a black man near his hometown. Three white men have been charged in connection with the slaying.

Pastor Charles Burchett, pastor of First Baptist Church of Kirbyville, led a prayer breakfast at the state Republican convention by confessing to the sin of racism and urging others in the overwhelmingly white crowd the same.

"Dear Lord, place the spirit of the Antichrist under the foot of Jesus," he prayed. "Forgive the white church in Texas for its sins".

His sermon, delivered to the tinkling of a piano on stage, was received with scattered cries of "hallelujah" and "amen" from the crown of about 400 that filled the John Fitzgerald Kennedy Theater at the Fort Worth Convention Center".

Chapter 12

The Chevron: a Shoulder Piece and a Reliable Key for Identifying the Key of David

The chevron emblem, which appears under terms of heraldry for the hashtag and which is worn upon the shoulders of noncommissioned officers and certain other government employees, is a key for identifying the Key of David. This key appears on the emblem of the US Great Seal, symbolizing that this key is what opens the US Great Seal and the national seals of its G7 partners. These are the seven seals from the 5th and 6th chapters of the book of Revelation. The pair of balances that appears also on the US Great Seal is symbolic of those balances described in Revelation 6:5 when the third seal is opened.

The key is positioned within a triangular figure along with the pair of balances to represent the third seal. In other words, the triangle symbolizes the number 3 for the third seal.

> And when he had opened the third seal, I heard the third beast say, Come and see. And I beheld, and lo a black horse; and he that sat on him had a pair of balances in his hand. (Rev. 6:5)

This chevron is symbolic of the chevron that constitutes the master mason compass needlepoints. When all the chevron veils are lifted, then it goes right back to Cleopatra's Needles as two candlesticks. Thus, it certifies itself as a reliable key for identifying the Key of David. It is the only key that can make a positive identification of the seven golden candlesticks.

Why is the chevron worn upon the shoulders of noncommissioned officers and other government workers? It alludes to a hidden Bible code for this key that has been identified and given only to God's messenger, Prophet Ellis. The phrase "upon his shoulder" is a repetitious Bible code that is used to allude to this stone, which is the keystone for the Key of David. I shall list several of them to show this revealing pattern of historical proportion.

> For unto us a child is born, unto us a son is given: and the government shall be upon his shoulder: and his name shall be called Wonderful, Counsellor, The mighty God, The everlasting Father, The Prince of Peace. (Isa. 9:6)

> And I will clothe him with thy robe, and strengthen him with thy girdle, and I will commit thy government into his hand: and he shall be a father to the inhabitants of Jerusalem, and to the house of Judah. And the key of the house of David will I lay upon his shoulder; so he shall open, and none shall shut; and he shall shut, and none shall open. (Isa. 22:21–22)

In preparation for this mystery of these great stones, God commanded Moses during the exodus, "Take two stones symbolic of Cleopatra's Needles, and place them on the priestly garments of his brother, Aaron, and his sons."

> And thou shalt take two onyx stones, and grave on them the names of the children of Israel: Six of their names on one stone, and the other six names of the rest on the other stone, according to their birth. And thou shalt put the two stones upon the shoulders of the ephod for stones of memorial

unto the children of Israel: and Aaron shall bear their names before the LORD upon his two shoulders for a memorial. (Exod. 28:9–10, 12)

The making of these cunning priestly garments and putting the stones upon the shoulder pieces of them were only a prelude to the twelve stones of memorial that was laid in the Jordan at Gilgal. It would be these twelve stones that would be raised as a pillar to become the Washington Memorial, holding the seven golden candlesticks. Here is God's command to Joshua when the people had passed over the Jordan.

> And it came to pass, when all the people were clean passed over Jordan, that the LORD spake unto Joshua, saying, Take you twelve men out of the people, out of every tribe a man, And command ye them, saying, Take you hence out of the midst of Jordan, out of the place where the priests' feet stood firm, twelve stones, and ye shall carry them over with you, and leave them in the lodging place, where ye shall lodge this night. [Note: this is the origin of the term Masonic Lodge.]
>
> Then Joshua called the twelve men, whom he had prepared of the children of Israel, out of every tribe a man: And Joshua said unto them, Pass over before the ark of the LORD your God into the midst of Jordan, and take you up every man of you a stone UPON HIS SHOULDER, according unto the number of the tribes of the children of Israel: That this may be a sign among you, that when your children ask their fathers in time to come, saying, What mean ye by these stones? Then ye shall answer them, That the waters of Jordan were cut off before the ark of the covenant of the LORD; when it passed over Jordan, the waters of Jordan were cut off: and these stones shall be for a memorial unto the children of Israel for ever.
>
> And the people came up out of Jordan on the tenth day of the first month, and encamped in Gilgal, in the east border of Jericho. (Josh. 4:1–7, 19)

Gilgal is a Hebrew term meaning circle of stones. This is where the Israelites crossed the Jordan and set up a memorial of twelve stones. It is written in Joshua 4:9 that these twelve stones are there until this day. This is a Bible code alluding to the fact that this memorial stands forever. These twelve stones have been raised as a pillar to become seven golden candlesticks, which is the Washington Memorial. These are the same stones that Jacob put for his pillows and set up for a pillar (Gen. 28:18–22). Jacob said this pillar shall be God's house, which we know is the Church. Jesus said in Revelation 1:20 that the mystery of the seven golden candlesticks is the seven churches. Prophet Ellis has proven that Jacob pillar is indeed the seven golden candlesticks.

In 1998, God would lead Prophet Ellis to Washington, D.C. to tour the Washington Memorial. During that trip, Prophet Ellis would collect for his prophetic library the *sightseeing* Washington Monument brochure, duplicated as an exhibit on the following page. God's spiritual gift to read symbolism and an understanding of dark sentences, which he gave to Prophet Ellis, enabled him to see a mystery on the brochure. The brochure would use symbolism to reveal that the twelve memorial stones of the Jordan were now hidden within the hollow walls of the Washington Monument.

Its designer would place a circle of twelve American flags around the monument to represent Gilgal, which means circle of stones. Each flag would have on it six stars to symbolize Gods' instruction to Moses for this memorial in Exodus 28:9–12. Six of the names of the children of Israel were placed on one stone and six names on the second stone, according to their birth. They were ordered to be memorials unto the Lord continually. The designer of the graphics for the brochure confirms this mystery.

There are, at the Washington Memorial, a circle of twelve stars representing the twelve tribes of Israel and the twelve memorial stones of the exodus. The circles of flags around the monument on the brochure are symbolic of Gilgal, which means circle of stones.

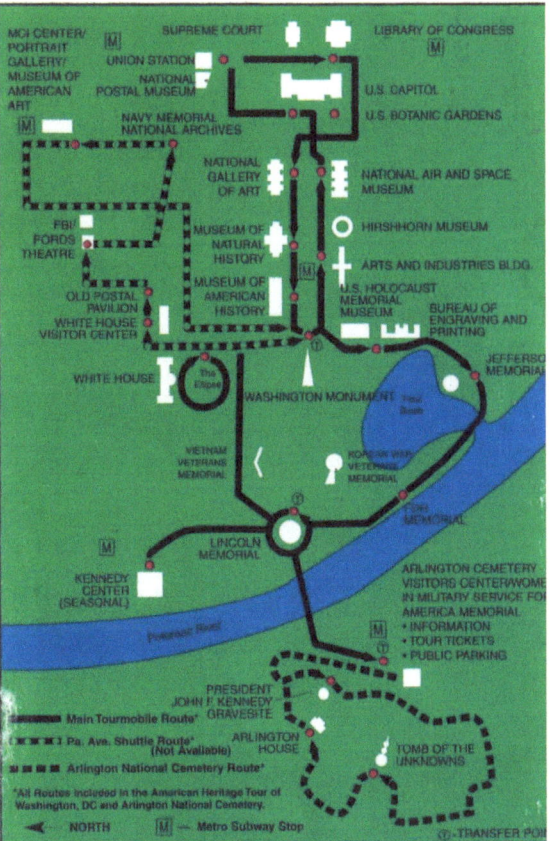

The Star of David composed of two interlaced Egyptian pyramid-like emblems would act as a sign and a key that God did all that is written and more when He delivered His people from Egyptian bondage. The two Egyptian pyramid-like triangles, which make the Star of David, represent the twin stone candlestick stone columns called Cleopatra's Needles. Therefore, the two equilateral delta triangles for the Star of David are also twins. Delta is the Greek alphabet which corresponds to the English *D* for the two *D*'s in the name David.

For over two hundred years, the Star of David has remained hidden on the US Great Seal, until God revealed its presence to Prophet Ellis. It was hidden by grouping twelve of the thirteen stars into the geometrical formation of the Star of David. It can be discerned only when the twelve stars are connected by straight lines, as shown on this page.

The Key of David graphics on this page appeared in the center of an October 8, 2005, editorial by Marvin Olasky, for *World Magazine*. There is nothing in the article about this key except ten coded words, saying, "The two columns a year, I try to write about Judaism."

Notes

RELATED ARTICLES:

The Washington Monument History …washingtondc.go.com/…washington-mon cool history of the Washington Monument provides information about the construction and designer.

Washington Monument Wikipedia, en.wikipedia.org/wiki/Washington-monument. The Washington Monument is an obelisk on the national Mall in Washington DC, built to the honor of George Washington.

Washington Monument completed Dec. 6, 1884—HISTORY.com

History And Facts Of The Washington Monument. www.essortment.com/history-washington: History and facts of the Washington monuments. A brief history behind the construction of the Washington Monument.

Washington Monument National Museum of American History…

Chapter 13

These Twelve Memorial Stones Are Now the Great Seal of the United States

The twelve memorial stones of Israel's exodus from Egyptian bondage became the Great Seal of the United States and the national seal of the United States' G7 partners. The twelve stones appear symbolically on the US one-dollar bill, where George Washington is positioned in the midst of them. "In the midst" means that Washington's image is positioned in the precise center of the one dollar bill.

When it is so placed, Washington is then symbolically in the midst of the seven golden candlesticks. The bills began with A-1 and ends with L-12. The Egyptian pyramid on the reverse side speaks softly of Egypt. God also revealed to Ellis the two candlesticks and the two olive branches on the bill. The two olive branches are behind the large number 1's at the top two corners along with a candlestick turned upside down in the upper right corner.

God left his signet in the earth with the nations to evidence their divine power to govern in His stead until the coming of the kingdom of God. The nations whom God had given power would identify God's messenger by the messenger's knowledge of this seal, which no man knows but he who receives it (Rev. 2:17). The five-pointed star on the seal is the same star which allowed King Herod to confirm the news of the birth of Jesus brought to him by the wise men from the east.

> Now when Jesus was born in Bethlehem of Judaea in the days of Herod the king, behold, there came wise men from the east to Jerusalem, Saying, Where is he that is born King of the Jews? for we have seen his star in the east, and are come to worship him. (Matt. 2:1–2)

God has revealed to Prophet Ellis things concerning the origin of the star on the US Great Seal, which no other human is privy. This star was hidden inside the apple at creation to evidence God's certificate of title to the earth, and that God is the Creator of both heaven and earth. This star can only be found by slicing the apple crosswise as a sign of our Savior's passion. David alluded to it in his prayer in Psalms 17:8. He asked the Lord to keep him as the apple of the eye. The mystery is alluded to also in Zechariah 2:8 where the Lord says, "For he that toucheth you toucheth the apple of the eye."

When Jacob poured oil and anointed this stone at Bethel, he was performing a ritual of the earth most golden secret (Gen. 28:18). God has revealed to Prophet Ellis the mystery of oil and how it is let down into the earth. It is the golden oil that the angel of the Lord showed unto Zechariah, which was flowing from the two olive branches.

> Then answered I, and said unto him, What are these two olive trees upon the right side of the candlestick and upon the left side thereof? (12) And I answered again, and said unto him, What be these two olive branches which through the two golden pipes empty the golden oil out of themselves? (Zech. 4:11–12)

God has revealed to Prophet Ellis that the funnel cloud of the tornado brings oil into the earth by a mystery. The chevron, which is one of the symbols of this stone, is what inspired the name for Chevron Oil and Gas. A chevron is made by dissecting an *x* into two equal parts. This inspired the name for Exxon oil and gas. This stone was given unto the United States when our union declared its independence in Philadelphia, Pennsylvania. This inspired the name for Pennzoil oil and gas, which use the Liberty Bell as a corporate emblem. This stone also inspired the nickname for Pennsylvania, which is called the Keystone State. Pennsylvania is also known as the Quaker State, thus, it inspired the name for Quaker State oil. This keystone also inspired the name for Keystone Pipeline oil.

This stone, being the pillar of our union, which was founded in 1776, also inspired the name for Union 76 oil. God allowed the first commercial oil well to be successfully drilled in Pennsylvania in 1859 by William Drake. This key opens and unseals the mysteries to all sixty-six books of the Bible. This spiritual truth inspired the name Phillips 66 oil and gas.

This keystone opens the golden doors to the largest oil and gas pipeline ever imagined. It has been hidden with the Antichrist. Oil, as Prophet Ellis has confirmed, has many biblical code names. It is called fire, which comes down from heaven by the wonders, and miracles, which the Antichrist has been given power to do. The world and all inhabitants of the earth have thus been deceived by the beast from the bottomless pit.

> And I beheld another beast coming up out of the earth; and he had two horns like a lamb, and he spake as a dragon.

> Note: these are the two horns on the Islamic crescent in heraldry, and they are the same two horns on ISIS's crown, which has a sun dial between them. Horns symbolize the power of these two candlesticks before the god of the earth. These two horns lead one to the seven golden candlesticks.

> And he exerciseth all the power of the first beast before him, and causeth the earth and them which dwell therein to worship the first beast, whose deadly wound was healed. And he doeth great wonders, so that he maketh fire come down from heaven on the earth in the sight of men, And deceiveth them that dwell on the earth by the means of those miracles which he had power to do in the sight of the beast. (Rev. 13:11–14)

Fire, honey, and wine are three biblical metaphors, which are used to hide and seal the mysteries of oil and gas. When the third seal is opened in the book of Revelation, the pair of balances on the US Great Seal, which sit above the chevron, are found with wine and oil.

> And when he had opened the third seal, I heard the third beast say, Come and see. And I beheld, and lo a black horse; and he that sat on him had a pair of balances in his hand. And I heard a voice in the midst of the four beasts say, A measure of wheat for a penny, and three measures of barley for a penny; and see thou hurt not the oil and the wine. (Rev. 6:5–6)

When an alcoholic guzzles wine like a gas-guzzling automobile, he becomes drunk. Therefore, the Bible describes the inhabitants of the earth as having been made drunk by the wine of the great whore, mystery Babylon.

> God is revealing this mystery so that those who have deceived His people may be judged at the opening of the national seals of those nations who call themselves the G7. These are the seven golden candlesticks that through their golden pipes, empty the golden oil out of themselves (Zech. 4:12).

> And there came one of the seven angels which had the seven vials, and talked with me, saying unto me, Come hither; I will shew unto thee the judgment of the great whore that sitteth upon many waters: With whom the kings of the earth have committed fornication, and the inhabitants of the earth have been made drunk with the wine of her fornication. (Rev. 17:1–2)

As this 17th chapter continues, oil is described as a harlot. And the tornado is described appropriately as the beast that carries her. A deep riddle alludes to the G7 and G8, as seven and eight kings, who own her, whom this chapter describes as the "mother of all harlots."

> And the angel said unto me, Wherefore didst thou marvel? I will tell thee the mystery of the woman, and of the beast that carrieth her, which hath the seven heads and ten horns. The beast that thou sawest was, and is not; and shall ascend out of the bottomless pit, and go into perdition: and they that dwell on the earth shall wonder, whose names were not written in the book of life from the foundation of the world, when they behold the beast that was, and is not, and yet is. (Rev. 17:7–8)

This riddle alludes to Russia who joined the G7, as the G8, but was expelled for invading the sovereignty of the Ukraine in 2013.

God hid these stones with the King of Babylon that his throne may be built up on them in the last days (Jer. 43:7–10).

> And say unto them, Thus saith the LORD of hosts, the God of Israel; Behold, I will send and take Nebuchadrezzar the king of Babylon, my servant, and will set his throne upon these stones that I have hid; and he shall spread his royal pavilion over them. (Jer. 43:10)

Jesus told the chief priests and Pharisees that whosoever shall fall on this stone shall be broken, but on whomsoever it shall fall, it will grind him to powder.

> Jesus saith unto them, Did ye never read in the scriptures, The stone which the builders rejected, the same is become the head of the corner: this is the Lord's doing, and it is marvellous in our eyes? Therefore say I unto you, The kingdom of God shall be taken from you, and given to a nation bringing forth the fruits thereof. And whosoever shall fall on this stone shall be broken: but on whomsoever it shall fall, it will grind him to powder. (Matt. 21:42–44)

The eighteenth chapter of Revelation shows that the same Babylon with whom God hid this stone that it is that same Babylon which falls on that stone. She falls when her oil carried in ships go up into smoke.

> And after these things I saw another angel come down from heaven, having great power; and the earth was lightened with his glory. And he cried mightily with a strong voice, saying, Babylon the great is fallen, is fallen, and is become the habitation of devils, and the hold of every foul spirit, and a cage of every unclean and hateful bird. For all nations have drunk of the wine of the wrath of her fornication, and the kings of the earth have committed fornication with her, and the merchants of the earth are waxed rich through the abundance of her delicacies.
>
> Therefore shall her plagues come in one day, death, and mourning, and famine; and she shall be utterly burned with fire: for strong is the Lord God who judgeth her. And the kings of the earth, who have committed fornication and lived deliciously with her, shall bewail her, and lament for her, when they shall see the smoke of her burning,
>
> Standing afar off for the fear of her torment, saying, Alas, alas that great city Babylon, that mighty city! for in one hour is thy judgment come. And the merchants of the earth shall weep and mourn over her; for no man buyeth their merchandise any more: The merchants of these things, which were made rich by her, shall stand afar off for the fear of her torment, weeping and wailing, And saying, Alas, alas that great city, that was clothed in fine linen, and purple, and scarlet, and decked with gold, and precious stones, and pearls! For in one hour so great riches is come to nought. And every shipmaster, and all the company in ships, and sailors, and as many as trade by sea, stood afar off, And cried when they saw the smoke of her burning, saying, What city is like unto this great city! (Rev. 18:1–3, 8–11, 15–18)

The final three verses of this 18th chapter allude to the fact that this stone and candlestick are one and the same.

> And a mighty angel took up a stone like a great millstone, and cast it into the sea, saying, Thus with violence shall that great city Babylon be thrown down, and shall be found no more at all. And the light of a candle shall shine no more at all in thee; and the voice of the bridegroom and of the bride shall be heard no more at all in thee: for thy merchants were the great men of the earth; for by thy sorceries were all nations deceived. And in her was found the blood of prophets, and of saints, and of all that were slain upon the earth. (Rev. 18:21, 23–24)

Notes

NOTE: Prophet Ellis's disclosures and public releases of the tornado clouds as the source of oil and gas into the earth; has inspired a new way for oil and gas exploration. It is being done quietly so that no attention may be focused on Ellis and his historical message.

www.oilgasmonitor.com/cloud-computing

Cloud Computing for Oil and Gas Companies (January 23, 2013) By: Michael Bennett—Edward Wildman Palmer LLP

What is Cloud Computing? Cloud computing has been characterized as a paradigm-shifting phenomenon that will change how we purchase IT resources and this is especially true for oil and gas companies.

Cloud computing is a loose term that describes a variety of data storage, processing and application services, normally provided by a third party using equipment not located on the customer's site.

True cloud services can be accessed, on demand, using a variety of readily available devices, such as computers with an Internet browser, Smart phones and tablets. Since the computing muscle resides in the cloud, the device used to access it can be relatively anemic and inexpensive.

RELATED ARTICLES: www.baselinemag.com The Technology of Oil Exploration BaselineMAG. May 5, 2006: Exxon looks to homegrown applications to gain a competitive advantage in oil exploration…

Why Cloud Computing is the Future of Oil & Gas Software. Info.drillinginfo.com/why-cloud…future-of…

Red Cloud Exploration: redcloudexploration.com It is this type of attitude and unrelenting focus that Red Cloud Exploration…leads his team in…

Most oil and gas companies plan to use cloud services…www.findingpetrolem.com/n/most…oil an…Introduction to Oil and Gas Exploration and…Most oil and gas companies plan to use cloud services…

SPECIAL NOTE: This is the great wonder how fire come down from heaven by the beast.

Chapter 14

Life Signified the Twelve Stones and Hashtag as Key to the Future

In its February 1989 special issue, *LIFE* magazine used symbolism predicting that the hashtag and these twelve memorial stones were the key to the future. It did this by using twelve birthstones in a circle that represented the twelve memorial stones that were laid at Gilgal. As I have illustrated earlier, *Gilgal* is a Hebrew word meaning circle of stones. Each stone was colored according to the birth of each tribe. At the top of the hashtag that represented the cross of our Lord's passion, the black stone is singled out as the one to watch as the year 2000 and beyond neared. The graphics were drawn by Nigel Holmes, a specialist in symbolism according to Prophet Ellis.

The graphics spoke by symbolism that this key of authority will be placed upon the shoulders of the black tribe of Israel. In other words, the Great Seal of the United States and the authority of it shall be passing to the black race. These things came to pass in 2008 when America elected its first African American president of Hebrew stock.

On the cover of the issue, *LIFE* man of the future, whose face was red, yellow, and blue, wore special soothsayer glasses of red and yellow. These colors represent the nature of the three who were crucified and those colors of the three crosses in the International Alphabet Flag Code.

On the inside cover was the Marlboro Man, which is a nickname given to the man Nebuchadnezzar, with whom God hid these stones. Also in the first few pages was the Masonic Bible on which George Washington was sworn into office on. The Bible was turned to the 49th and 50th chapters of Genesis, whereby Jacob blessed each of his twelve sons and predicted the future of each tribe. It is the Masonic Bible that President George Herbert Bush had been sworn in to office on just a few weeks earlier. The oath of office on a Masonic Bible binds the president to Masonic doctrines and beliefs.

Who is *LIFE* magazine that they are privy to these deep mysteries regarding these twelve memorial stones and the hashtag? That question was answered by *LIFE*'s reporters in a special June 2012 issue of *LIFE* on "The Hidden World of Secret Societies," according to records in Prophet Ellis's library. It is clear that *LIFE* had come in contact with Prophet Ellis's prophetic writings and revelations and saw a need to quickly debunk them. Therefore, this special issue of *LIFE* purports to investigate all secret societies and expose them. "Exposed!" appeared throughout the issue as they did nothing more than recite a brief history of each organization, and after doing so, they attempt to say in their conclusion, "See, there is nothing there, it's all a conspiracy theory." But how can the world debunk God's Word and His anointed?

On its last page, the reporters entered something, perhaps jokingly, which they said could get them fired. Prophet Ellis was able to use those revelations to illustrate *LIFE*'s interest in the hashtag and twelve memorial stones as being the key to the future.

On its last page, on secret societies, the same being page 119, *LIFE* revealed a bombshell about its founder, Henry Robinson Luce. *LIFE* wrote, just before revealing this bombshell, these words, saying, "Running this as our last page could (or might) get the staff of *LIFE* books fired." They continued with a question, saying, "What is it?"

It is a super-secret roster of the 1920 class of Yale's Skull and Bones. Listed, you will find Henry Luce and Briton Hadden, who are also editorial colleagues on *Yale Daily News*. Upon graduating, they will team up and cofound *TIME* magazine. Luce will go on to found *Fortune* and then *LIFE*. And our company will spin on and on and merge with Warner Communications, Inc., and then do that silly AOL thing and, "Did Luce and Hadden plot all this in the recesses of the tomb in New Haven? We cannot say, really we cannot say."

The tomb in New Haven is a clue to the tomb, which Prophet Ellis has unveiled as Masonry's Mystic Shrine, an ancient Islamic plot to use the Skull and Bones of another person, and present these in the last days as the Skull and Bones of Jesus. The number 322, which is the number that is associated with the Skull and Bones fraternity, is a cryptic reference to the hashtag, which depicts how Jesus's apron was divided by the soldiers who crucified him.

TIME as in TIME/LIFE, New York Times, Los Angeles Times, and many others are Masonic terms for the Greek god, Kronos, who is also called Cronus. He is also called Saturn whose emblem is the sickle. It is the same sickle used by Lenin, the founder of the Soviet Union, and the same sickle seen in 14th chapter of Revelation during the day of harvest, it being the same as the crescent as used by Islam.

Prophet Ellis has among his library a 1927 Freemasonry training book with 1001 questions and answers. It is titled *Ask Me Brother*, but it is called *A Thousand Points of Light* by ranking Freemasons. In its general test number twenty-one and question number 5, ask as follows: "How does Kronos or time appear in the Masonic system?" The answer is one that a wise man would examine closely. The answer states: "In the emblem of the beautiful Virgin weeping beside a broken columns, where Kronus is seen pointing to the summit of the zodiacal arch."

The broken column refers to Cleopatra's Needle and the opening of the seven seal. Cleopatra is worshiped as ISIS by Egyptians and others. She is portrayed as the Virgin Mary both by Masonry and the Vatican. This is confirmed by general test number twenty-eight under Q&A fifteen.

Notes

RELATED ARTICLES: Cronus on Greek Mythology

www.greekmythology.com/titans/cronus/...

KRONOS (or Cronus) was the Titan god of time and the ages, especially time regarded as destructive.

Saturn (mythology) – Wikipedia, en.m.wikipedia.org/wiki/Saturn. (mythology)

Mythology of /Saturn. The Romans identified Saturn with the Greek Cronus, whose myths were adapted for...

Saturn (Latin: Saturnus) is a god in ancient Roman religion, and a character in myth. Saturn is a complex figure because of his multiple associations and long history. He was the first god of the Capitol, known since the most ancient times as Saturnius Mons, and was seen as a god of generation, dissolution, plenty, wealth, agriculture, periodic renewal and liberation In later developments he came to be also a god of time. His reign was depicted as a Golden Age of plenty and peace.

The Temple of Saturn in the Roman Forum housed the state treasury. In December, he was celebrated at what is perhaps the most famous of the Roman festivals, the Saturnalia, a time of feasting, role reversals, free speech, gift-giving and revelry. Saturn the planet and Saturday are both named after the god.

OTHER RELATED SOURCES:

PROPHESY: Key to The Future: Duane S. Crowther 9789882907819

www.amazon.com/prophesy-key-to-the-future

Chapter 15

Cleopatra's Needle Certifies the Resurrection of King David as America's 44th President

Prophet Ellis is able and has shown that these two candlesticks were shown to the prophet Ezekiel in a vision in the "Valley of Dry Bones." It is a vision where God showed him the resurrection of both Israel and King David.

> Blessed and holy is he that hath part in the first resurrection: on such the second death hath no power, but they shall be priests of God and of Christ, and shall reign with him a thousand years. And when the thousand years are expired, Satan shall be loosed out of his prison, And shall go out to deceive the nations which are in the four quarters of the earth, Gog, and Magog, to gather them together to battle: the number of whom is as the sand of the sea. (Rev. 20:6–8)

God showed unto the prophet Ezekiel this great vision of the resurrection of Israel and King David in a vision whereby it is chronicled in the 37th chapter of Ezekiel. The vision and prophesy are divided into two parts. The first part is the vision of the dry bones and Israel's resurrection. The second part are the two candlesticks from Egypt that are joined together to make one stick as the sign of a kingdom where David is king forever. It is a scripture that requires much more than academic intellect to discern. It can only be spiritually discerned by the power of the Holy Ghost. It is indeed a mystery. It is for that reason God put forth his question to his prophet Ezekiel, asking him, "Son of man can these bones live?" Ezekiel did not answer yes or no. Rather, he simply said, "O Lord GOD, thou knowest."

It is important to know that this is a resurrection in the flesh and not the spirit. This illustration is critical because God has not only raised the house of Israel and Judah, but He raised King David as the 44th US president as prophesied by both Ezekiel and Jeremiah.

There will be many who will doubt this for the sake of expediency. It is for this reason that God has called the two candlesticks His two witnesses (Rev. 11:1–19). They are the sign of the resurrection and they shall be resurrected before the eyes of all nations after being killed by the beast to be raised by God. In the 24th chapter of Joshua in verse 27, Joshua called all of Israel and said, "These stones shall be a witness unto Israel, lest it deny its God." The resurrection is shown in these following scriptures, saying:

> Again he said unto me, Prophesy upon these bones, and say unto them, O ye dry bones, hear the word of the LORD. Thus saith the Lord GOD unto these bones; Behold, I will cause breath to enter into you, and ye shall live: And I will lay sinews upon you, and will bring up flesh upon you, and cover you with skin, and put breath in you, and ye shall live; and ye shall know that I am the LORD.
>
> So I prophesied as I was commanded: and as I prophesied, there was a noise, and behold a shaking, and the bones came together, bone to his bone. And when I beheld, lo, the sinews and the flesh came up upon them, and the skin covered them above: but there was no breath in them. Then said he unto me, Prophesy unto the wind, prophesy, son of man, and say to the wind, Thus saith the Lord GOD; Come from the four winds, O breath, and breathe upon these slain, that they may live.
>
> So I prophesied as he commanded me, and the breath came into them, and they lived, and stood up upon their feet, an exceeding great army. Then he said unto me, Son of man, these bones are the

whole house of Israel: behold, they say, Our bones are dried, and our hope is lost: we are cut off for our parts. (Ezek. 37:4–11)

In the second part, the Lord would take Ezekiel through a strange ritual with two sticks representing Cleopatra's Needles. The Egyptian origin would be coded by the Lord, calling it Joseph's stick in the hand of his Egyptian son, Ephraim. Then God would call them one stick in his hand. These are the seven golden candlesticks that are seen in the Lord's right hand in Revelation 1:20. They are joined as the Washington Monument into one stick in the Lord's hand.

The word of the LORD came again unto me, saying, Moreover, thou son of man, take thee one stick, and write upon it, For Judah, and for the children of Israel his companions: then take another stick, and write upon it, For Joseph, the stick of Ephraim and for all the house of Israel his companions: And join them one to another into one stick; and they shall become one in thine hand. And when the children of thy people shall speak unto thee, saying, Wilt thou not shew us what thou meanest by these? Say unto them, Thus saith the Lord GOD; Behold, I will take the stick of Joseph, which is in the hand of Ephraim, and the tribes of Israel his fellows, and will put them with him, even with the stick of Judah, and make them one stick, and they shall be one in mine hand. (Ezek. 37:15–19)

God had Ezekiel to write upon these sticks so that another biblical code would be left verifying them as what we call Cleopatra's Needles. These are the same candlesticks that Moses symbolically wrote the names of the children of Israel. Six of their names were written on one stone and the names of the other six on the second stone (Exod. 28:9–12).

And the sticks whereon thou writest shall be in thine hand before their eyes. And say unto them, Thus saith the Lord GOD; Behold, I will take the children of Israel from among the heathen, whither they be gone, and will gather them on every side, and bring them into their own land: And I will make them one nation in the land upon the mountains of Israel; and one king shall be king to them all: and they shall be no more two nations, neither shall they be divided into two kingdoms any more at all. Neither shall they defile themselves any more with their idols, nor with their detestable things, nor with any of their transgressions: but I will save them out of all their dwelling places, wherein they have sinned, and will cleanse them: so shall they be my people, and I will be their God.

And David my servant shall be king over them; and they all shall have one shepherd: they shall also walk in my judgments, and observe my statutes, and do them. And they shall dwell in the land that I have given unto Jacob my servant, wherein your fathers have dwelt; and they shall dwell therein, even they, and their children, and their children's children for ever: and my servant David shall be their prince forever.

Moreover I will make a covenant of peace with them; it shall be an everlasting covenant with them: and I will place them, and multiply them, and will set my sanctuary in the midst of them for evermore. And the heathen shall know that I the LORD do sanctify Israel, when my sanctuary shall be in the midst of them for evermore. (Ezek. 37:20–26, 28)

These two candlesticks are therefore the key to certifying and verifying both the resurrection of David and also the resurrection of the whole house of Israel. It is a resurrection in the flesh. What is the purpose of two resurrections and the resurrection of the whole house of Israel? So that all those who died before the coming of a Savior would have an equal chance to receive or reject God's grace and forgiveness of sins. This key is therefore appropriately called the key to the house of David. The key is the symbolic cornerstone for the Lord's sanctuary that is to be built in America. It will be built in the new promise land. Old Jerusalem has been defiled with bloodshed spreading over many centuries. All the bloodshed in the Middle East today stems from the controversy over the Temple Mount and the anticipation of the rebuilding of God's sanctuary. Therefore, God has created a new earth and a New Jerusalem, which men call the New World. Here, David will be our prince forever.

This mystery is further corroborated by the symbolism of the two equilateral triangles, which makes up the Star of David, and are hidden on the US Great Seal. These two triangles are the Greek alphabet delta, which corresponds to our English *D*, for the two *D*'s in David. *D* has an alphabet numerical place value of 4. Therefore, when the two are interlaced together, they represent the number 44 for America's 44th president.

God said to Ezekiel that David shall be prince forever. It was this prophetic truth that inspired the US Postal Service to speak by symbolism with the printing of a 44¢ forever stamp. It was printed only after the 44th US president was sworn into office.

News organizations and opponents of the forty-fourth US president are careful to use only deft symbolism when communicating his King David identity. On January 17, 2012, the *UK Daily Mail Reporter* used an original and a parody version of Donald Trump's family crest to depict the forty-fourth US president as the unwelcome resurrected King David. The online article related to the Court victory won by Trump from the Scottish heralds to use his family crest at his newly opened golf course in Scotland. The Trump family crest can be seen as an original version of the Keystone, which opens the US Great Seal. Two identical chevrons represent the twin pillars known as Cleopatra's Needles. Their precise height is a key that opens the US Great Seal and the national seals of its G7 industrialized partners. Thus, they are called keystones.

This is the same keystone that God used to reveal Jesus to Peter, prompting Jesus to give Peter these keys to the kingdom of heaven (Matthew16:13–19).

What is the Trump family crest saying through its symbolism? The one lion below the two chevrons in the key position represents Jesus, who is the lion of the tribe of Judah. It is he who opens the seven seals. "And one of the elders saith unto me, Weep not: behold, the Lion of the triba of Juda, the Root of David, hath prevailed to open the book, and to loose the seven seals thereof" (Revelation 5:5).

Exactly eight symbolic stone pillars are fixed beneath the two chevrons where the lion sits in the keystone position. These eight stone pillars represent eight times the 69.375-foot height of Cleopatra's Needles that gives you a height equal to the 555-foot height of the Washington Monument.

The two lions at the top of the crest with the thirteen stone pillars represent Trump's paternal and maternal grandparents. Trump's paternal grandfather was Fredrick Christ Trump of Germany. His maternal grandfather was Christ Christ of Scotland. These two are symbolic of the two beasts in the thirteenth chapter of Revelation who are the antichrist.

The thirteen stone pillars above the chevrons plus the eight that are below the chevrons are equal to twenty-one. The two on the left and right of the two chevrons simply represent the two twin pillars called Cleopatra's Needles. These twenty-one pillars are what inspired the gambling game that is called twenty-one poker. Poker is the name given to the soldier who pierced our Lord Jesus. *Poke* simply means "to push against with something pointed." The terms of heraldry illustrate by numbers the places where Jesus was pierced. The Honor point is 10 and the Nombril point is 11, whose sum is 21.

Jack is a Hebrew name. It means "gracious gift of God." Jesus was called blackjack. The soldier who pierced him was called the blackjack poker. The casino was introduced by Pope Julius III, who was called the evilest of all popes. The parody version of Trump's coat of arms follows the path of Pope Julius III by placing Trump's casino upon the symbolic rock where Jesus said he would build his church and the gates of hell shall not prevail against it. The forty-fourth president's birth certificate is placed in the key position and is knocked out of its place with a Donald Trump iron fist. Beneath it is the Latin phrase "Ego te demitto." Its English translation means "You are fired."

The two combs represent the measuring bars on the master mason's square. The two girls represent the twin pillars called Cleopatra's Needles. They are identical and symbolic of the pair of balances seen when the third seal is opened. "And when he had opened the third seal, I heard the third beast say, Come and see. And I beheld, and lo, a black horse; and he that sat on him had a pair of balances in his hand" (Revelation 6:5).

The US possession of these Egyptian pillars that bring on the horses of the apocalypse inspired the name of a champion racehorse that is named American Pharaoh. When God neutralized the power of this keystone, He sent GOP 2016 presidential ambitions into total chaos and confusion.

Notes

Related Articles: King David's Resurrection? From Yahoo Answers

The purpose of the millennium is for Jesus to restore everything, including man, to perfection. Those of us who are still alive after Armageddon will have the privilege of teaching those resurrected the truth about God and what they must do to continue to live forever. David will no longer be a king but he will have no difficulty adjusting to the new world. He was a shining example of……full answer

Achorian Bible A Prophesy: www.achorian.com/kingdavid.html

These scriptures reveal there is a book of life from which Jesus Christ will resurrect His believers when…

Will David reign with Jesus in the Millennial Kingdom?

www.gotquestions.org/david-kingdom.html

Do the prophecies in Ezekiel mean that King David will literally…God and David their King…that…,

Where will David be in the resurrection? –JW info line

www.winfoline.com/documents/resurrection…

Act 2:34 say that David did not ascent into heaven. Why? Acts chapter 2 describes David's prophecy…

FulfiledProphesy.com*View topic – King David will reign in…

King David will reign in Jerusalem under…David their king, who will be resurrected…

King David's Role In The Millennium—Bible Track

www.bibletrack.org/notes/resources/misc/D…

…King David will reign in Jerusalem under Jesus…and David their king…he will be resurrected.

Chapter 16

Phi Beta Kappa Golden Key Represents the Key of David

It was only six months after the United States received this keystone and declared its independence at Philadelphia, Pennsylvania, that the fraternity of Phi Beta Kappa was established at the College of William and Mary. It was on December 5, 1776. It would be an offshoot of Freemasonry, and most of its new members, if not all, would be Freemasons. The golden key given to the new members would not be just any old golden key. Their key uses symbolism that challenged the brightest of the brightest to decipher their meaning. Doing so would require one with the means to slip into the golden gates of heaven and burglarize the chambers of God's vaults for its most golden secret. As of this day, there is no record anyone having accomplished this insurmountable task.

Phi Beta Kappa was the first college or university fraternity organized in the new colonies. When Greek letters and the Latin language are used among a people who speak only English, then it is a reasonable bet that the person or people are up to something clever.

The keystone that God has given unto Prophet Ellis, which he has shown, is in fact the Key of David and has opened and unsealed the mysteries of the Phi Beta Kappa golden key. He has proven and articulated that it is symbolic of the keystone that was given by God's favor to the

United States just six months earlier. Members of the Skull and Bones society are most likely to be members of the Phi Beta Kappa fraternity.

It is highly unlikely new members would know the purpose and basis upon which the organization was founded. It is possible that some may have received a glimmer of light into the fraternity's dark chambers, but its golden secrets were not written down for future generations. These secrets are hidden beneath many symbolic veils of the order of Freemasonry.

The symbols on the Phi Beta Kappa golden key is a book representing the Holy Bible, three stars representing Jesus, and the two malefactors who were crucified with him, and a right hand representing that the book is in the right hand of the Father. The Greek *Phi* corresponds to the English "ph," which has the sound of "fa" for "Father," representing God the Father.

The Greek *Beta* corresponds to the English *B*, and the Greek *Kappa* corresponds to the English *K*. The "BK" is combined as the abbreviation for *book*. Therefore, the complete translation of Phi-Beta-Kappa along with the other symbols is "book in the right hand of the father." The book is the Bible, and the golden key, which is the Key of David, is the key that unseals that book. These are the biblical seven seals which are the national seals of the United States and its G7 partners. These are the seven golden candlesticks.

The symbol for the Phi Beta Kappa golden key is a conversion of plain biblical text into complex symbolism. Here is that biblical text.

> And I saw in the right hand of him that sat on the throne a book written within and on the backside, sealed with seven seals. (Rev. 5:1)

What are the seven seals in the right hand?

> The mystery of the seven stars which thou sawest in my right hand, and the seven golden candlesticks. The seven stars are the angels of the seven churches: and the seven candlesticks which thou sawest are the seven churches. (Rev. 1:20)

This key has opened a golden door in heaven. When that door is opened, this stone, which is called the keystone, is revealed as Jesus Christ. Therefore, to look upon this stone is to look upon he who has given unto Prophet Ellis, the white stone of the promise. Dr. Martin Luther King has called it the stone of hope. That door has now been opened to reveal the throne of David. Upon that throne is one who looks like a jasper and a sardine stone. That stone is a proxy for Jesus's power in all the earth.

> After this I looked, and, behold, a door was opened in heaven: and the first voice which I heard was as it were of a trumpet talking with me; which said, Come up hither, and I will shew thee things which must be hereafter. And immediately I was in the spirit: and, behold, a throne was set in heaven, and one sat on the throne. And he that sat was to look upon like a jasper and a sardine stone: and there was a rainbow round about the throne, in sight like unto an emerald. (Rev. 4:1–3)

> And I saw a strong angel proclaiming with a loud voice, Who is worthy to open the book, and to loose the seals thereof? And no man in heaven, nor in earth, neither under the earth, was able to open the book, neither to look thereon. And I wept much, because no man was found worthy to open and to read the book, neither to look thereon. And one of the elders saith unto me, Weep not: behold, the Lion of the tribe of Judah, the Root of David, hath prevailed to open the book, and to loose the seven seals thereof. (Rev. 5:2–5)

This is the mystery of the Phi Beta Kappa golden key. It is the Key of David that has now opened the United States and the G7 national seals.

Notes

Related Articles:

Phi-Beta-Kappa – History–index of Student Organizations

www.clubs.psu.edu/phibetakappa.appa/hist.htm

The History Phi Beta Kappa. The Founding of Phi Beta Kappa. Phi Beta Kappa was founded on December 5, 1776

Phi Beta Kappa National Honor Society–PBK Home

www.pbk.org

The faces behind the key features Phi Beta Kappa members whose lives have been shaped by…

A Brief History of Phi Beta Kappa–

PBK Home

www.pbk.org/imisi5/pbk. Member/About…

Phi Beta Kappa was founded by five students at the College of William and Mary in Williamsburg, Virginia. The first meeting was held in the Apollo Room of the Old Raleigh Tavern on December 5, 1776.

John Heath, the first president of Phi Beta Kappa, was determined to develop a student society that would be much more serious minded than its predecessors at the college. One devoted to the pursuit of liberal education and intellectual fellowship. The Greek initials for the society's motto, "Love of learning is the guide of life," form the name Phi Beta Kappa.

The first college society to bear a Greek-letter name. Phi-Beta-Kappa introduced the essential characteristics of the Greek societies that followed it: an oath of secrecy, a badge, mottoes in Greek and Latin, a code of laws, an elaborate form of initiation, a seal, and a special handshake. The organization was created as a secret society so that its founders would have the freedom to discuss any topic they chose. Freedom of inquiry has been a hallmark of Phi-Beta-Kappa ever since.

Chapter 17

The United States' Inherent Obligation to Build the Lord's Temple in America

Most of the global terror and violence from the so-called Islamic extremists are centered around the Holy Site in Jerusalem, which is called the Temple Mount. It is the place where Jews, Christians, and Islam have all anticipated as the place of the latter temple of God. Likewise, Prophet Ellis assumed that the latter house was to be rebuilt on the site that is believed to be the original site of former temples. Today, that site is occupied by the Islamic shrine called Dome of the Rock. It is all but certain that this shrine was built there to prevent the construction and rebuilding of the latter temple. It was built by the Freemasons for Islam and has been there for more than 1300 years.

Today, as Israel feel threaten by what it believes is Iran's ambition to build nuclear weapons capable of destroying Israel, all are searching for a peaceful solution. Just the mention of the phrase "Millennium Temple" is enough to set off a string of violence that has happen all too often. Now that the New Earth and the New Jerusalem is made known, such a revelation has also revealed the site of the latter house of God.

Old Jerusalem has had all her glory and striking beauty defiled by hatred and bloodshed through many centuries of violence. As ISIS and Al Qaeda anticipate that the time has come to rebuild God's house, they have therefore swung into action with great violence on Christians and Jews alike. But God has promised peace in this latter house.

> The glory of this latter house shall be greater than of the former, saith the Lord of hosts: and in this place will I give peace, saith the Lord of hosts. (Hag. 2:9)

> And speak unto him, saying, Thus speaketh the Lord of hosts, saying, Behold the man whose name is The Branch; and he shall grow up out of his place, and he shall build the temple of the Lord: Even he shall build the temple of the Lord; and he shall bear the glory, and shall sit and rule upon his throne; and he shall be a priest upon his throne: and the counsel of peace shall be between them both. (Zech. 6:12–13)

> And there shall come forth a rod out of the stem of Jesse, and a Branch shall grow out of his roots: And righteousness shall be the girdle of his loins, and faithfulness the girdle of his reins. The wolf also shall dwell with the lamb, and the leopard shall lie down with the kid; and the calf and the young lion and the fatling together; and a little child shall lead them. And the cow and the bear shall feed; their young ones shall lie down together: and the lion shall eat straw like the ox. And the sucking child shall play on the hole of the asp, and the weaned child shall put his hand on the cockatrice' den. They shall not hurt nor destroy in all my holy mountain: for the earth shall be full of the knowledge of the Lord, as the waters cover the sea. (Isa. 11:1, 5–9)

When the Nobel Peace Prize was awarded to President Obama before he took office, the Nobel committee was looking at the prophetic scripture; for Prophet Ellis had already identified him as King David from his manuscript titled *Upon This Rock*. *Upon This Rock* chronicles the history of this stone from Bethel to the swearing in of Barack Obama as the 44th president of the United States.

The prophet Isaiah gives a hopeful preview of how all the children of Abraham, who have been fighting against one another for thousands of years, are now joined together in a lasting peace and an unbreakable bond of love and brotherhood. But where is the place of the Lord rest?

In February 1887, a special tract of land was purchased by the grandparents of Prophet Ellis, where the Lord has ordered His temple to be built. The United States and its G7 industrialized partners, whom God has favored, has an inherent obligation to rebuild the temple of God. The Freemasons statement in their profile of the 16° (degree) as prince of Jerusalem strongly suggest that they are aware of this obligation. They have stated that they no longer expect to rebuild the temple at Jerusalem. They go on to state, "No longer needing to repair to Jerusalem to worship, nor to offer up sacrifices and shed blood to propitiate the Deity." Prophet Ellis has said with all due respect to the Freemasons, "They did not say that they would not build the Lord's house." They said that they do not plan to rebuild in Jerusalem. The land, on which it is to be rebuilt, has been well marked by a mystery to certify that the land is for that purpose. Here is how it was marked according to Prophet Ellis.

It is located in a survey that was named during the Spanish land grant after one of the twenty-four elders. These elders are in Revelation 5:5, which says, "And one of the elders saith unto me, Weep not: behold, the Lion of the tribe of Judah, the Root of David, hath prevailed to open the book, and to loose the seven seals thereof."

An identity of these twenty-four elders has remained an unsolved mystery until God unsealed them with the Key of David and revealed them to Prophet Ellis. All twenty-four of the elders who had twelve sons each were directly associated with King David. They were David's musicians who provided the services for the house of God. The thirteenth of the twenty-four was Shubael. The tract of land is located in what is called "Shubael Marsh." The original deed was recorded in "T-13" for the thirteenth elder Shubael.

I have not found any record of any school of theology, clergymen, scholars, or any natural person, who has identified and published the names of the twenty-four elders in the book of Revelation. Therefore, I have concluded that Prophet Ellis's positive and corroborated identification of these twenty-four elders has come only by the divine revelations of God. The church at Rome has incorrectly identified these elders as the twelve tribes of Israel and the twelve apostles. Prophet Ellis has correctly identified them as King David's musicians whom God has now raised up in the resurrection to perform the same services around the throne of David, which they also performed in the sanctuary of David. They appear around the throne harping with their harps, praising and worshipping God. One of these twenty-four elders has been identified by Prophet Ellis as one of the greatest pop singers of the twenty-first century. Each elder had twelve sons who were ordered by David to prophesy with their harps, psalteries, and cymbals. All the twenty-four are named in the 25th chapter of 1 Chronicles, and one declared Jesus as worthy to open the seven seals. This elder has been identified as Shubael whom God has raised up as a sign among us today.

> Moreover David and the captains of the host separated to the service of the sons of Asaph, and of Heman, and of Jeduthun, who should prophesy with harps, with psalteries, and with cymbals: So the number of them, with their brethren that were instructed in the songs of the LORD, even all that were cunning, was two hundred fourscore and eight. And they cast lots, ward against ward, as well the small as the great, the teacher as the scholar. Now the first lot came forth for Asaph to Joseph: the second to Gedaliah, who with his brethren and sons were twelve: The third to Zaccur, The fourth to Izri, The fifth to Nethaniah, The sixth to Bukkiah, The seventh to Jesharelah, The eighth to Jeshaiah, The ninth to Mattaniah, The tenth to Shimei, The eleventh to Azareel, The twelfth to Hashabiah, The thirteenth to Shubael, The fourteenth to Mattithiah, The fifteenth to Jeremoth, The sixteenth to Hananiah, The seventeenth to Joshbekashah, The eighteenth to Hanani, The nineteenth to Mallothi, The twentieth to Eliathah, The one and twentieth to Hothir, The two and twentieth to Giddalti, The three and twentieth to Mahazioth, The four and twentieth to Romamtiezer. (1 Chron. 25:1, 7–31)

It is a mystery in itself for twenty-four men to have twelve sons each such as Jacob, the father of the twelve tribes of Israel. They were all gifted and cunning in their art. David ordered them to prophesy with their harps. These elders are associated with the opening of the seven seals, which are the substance of the seven golden candlesticks. They appear as singers with their harps around the throne of God where the stone also appear.

> And immediately I was in the spirit: and, behold, a throne was set in heaven, and one sat on the throne. And he that sat was to look upon like a jasper and a sardine stone: and there was a rainbow round about the throne, in sight like unto an emerald. And round about the throne were four and twenty seats: and upon the seats I saw four and twenty elders sitting, clothed in white raiment; and they had on their heads crowns of gold. And out of the throne proceeded lightnings and thunderings and voices: and there were seven lamps of fire burning before the throne, which are the seven Spirits of God. And before the throne there was a sea of glass like unto crystal: and in the midst of the throne, and round about the throne, were four beasts full of eyes before and behind. And when those beasts give glory and honour and thanks to him that sat on the throne, who liveth for ever and ever, The four and twenty elders fall down before him that sat on the throne, and worship him that liveth for ever and ever, and cast their crowns before the throne, saying, Thou art worthy, O Lord, to receive glory and honour and power: for thou hast created all things, and for thy pleasure they are and were created. (Rev. 4:2–6, 9–11)

One of the main purposes of the two candlesticks stone pillars is to bear witness that God did create all things for His pleasure and for His glory. Therefore, one of the twenty-four elders will declare Jesus as the sacrificial Lamb who is the only one worthy to open the seven seals, which evidence God's creation. This continues in the 5th chapter of Revelation as the mystery of the twenty-four elders gradually is revealed by God to Prophet Ellis.

> And I saw in the right hand of him that sat on the throne a book written within and on the backside, sealed with seven seals. And I saw a strong angel proclaiming with a loud voice, Who is worthy to open the book, and to loose the seals thereof? And no man in heaven, nor in earth, neither under the earth, was able to open the book, neither to look thereon. And I wept much, because no man was found worthy to open and to read the book, neither to look thereon.
>
> And one of the elders saith unto me, Weep not: behold, the Lion of the tribe of Judah, the Root of David, hath prevailed to open the book, and to loose the seven seals thereof. And I beheld, and, lo, in the midst of the throne and of the four beasts, and in the midst of the elders, stood a Lamb as it had been slain, having seven horns and seven eyes, which are the seven Spirits of God sent forth into all the earth. And he came and took the book out of the right hand of him that sat upon the throne. And when he had taken the book, the four beasts and four and twenty elders fell down before the Lamb, having every one of them harps, and golden vials full of odours, which are the prayers of saints. And they sung a new song, saying, Thou art worthy to take the book, and to open the seals thereof: for thou wast slain, and hast redeemed us to God by thy blood out of every kindred, and tongue, and people, and nation; And hast made us unto our God kings and priests: and we shall reign on the earth. And the four beasts said, Amen. And the four and twenty elders fell down and worshipped him that liveth for ever and ever. (Rev. 5:1–10, 14)

As the mystery of the twenty-four elders is revealed, it is essential that special attention is given to their association with God's two witnesses and the building of the temple of God. They all come together with the death and resurrection of God's two witnesses, who are killed by the Antichrist. These are the two candlesticks and two olive trees in Revelation chapter 11, where the elders are worshipping God after a great victory over the kingdoms of this world.

> And the seventh angel sounded; and there were great voices in heaven, saying, The kingdoms of this world are become the kingdoms of our Lord, and of his Christ; and he shall reign for ever and ever. And the four and twenty elders, which sat before God on their seats, fell upon their faces, and

worshipped God, Saying, We give thee thanks, O LORD God Almighty, which art, and wast, and art to come; because thou hast taken to thee thy great power, and hast reigned.

And the nations were angry, and thy wrath is come, and the time of the dead, that they should be judged, and that thou shouldest give reward unto thy servants the prophets, and to the saints, and them that fear thy name, small and great; and shouldest destroy them which destroy the earth. And the temple of God was opened in heaven, and there was seen in his temple the ark of his testament: and there were lightnings, and voices, and thunderings, and an earthquake, and great hail. (Rev. 11:15–19)

The new temple that was opened in heaven is that temple shown to the prophet Ezekiel beginning with chapter 40 and verse number 1. God had men to go before Prophet Ellis in a mystery to prepare the way for the place of His temple. God had prepared it in such a manner so that no rational person can honestly doubt it as being the orders of God.

According to the real estate and deed records for the Brazoria County Clerk's Office in Angleton, Texas, it all began on July 17, 1824. On this date, the Mexican government would grant a league of land containing 1107 acres to Shubael Marsh. Shubael is the thirteenth of the twenty-four elders who are named and numbered in 1 Chronicles chapter 25. Shubael Marsh, to whom this property was conveyed, was one of Stephen F. Austin's Old Three Hundred colonists. According to Texas historical records, Shubael Marsh was born in Portland, Maine, and died in 1868.

On February 9, 1881, some two hundred acres of his land would pass to James Caruthers who would pass it to Prophet Ellis's grandparents shortly thereafter. It appears that James Caruthers purchased it solely for that purpose. The records of the County Clerk would have hidden within it a divine message which only God's messenger could find and decipher by the counsel of the Holy Spirit. This transaction began just as Cleopatra's Needle had been moved to New York Central Park, and work had gotten underway with building the Washington Monument. The Washington Monument is the substance of the seven seals and the seven golden candlesticks.

In order that the deed records encrypt Shubael as the thirteenth of the twenty-four elders found in 1 Chronicles 25 at verse 20, their deed was recorded in book T-page 13. The 13th represented 1 Chronicles which is the thirteenth book of the Bible. And it also represented the thirteenth of the twenty-four elders. The letter *T*, which is the twentieth English alphabet, represented the 20th verse.

The plat records of the land in the County Clerk Office would also have the name Shubael written in a special way to allude to him as being one of the twenty-four elders. To accomplish this, the surveyor of the land would place the twenty-fourth English alphabet *X* under the last two letters *EL* in the name Shubael. *EL* is the abbreviation for elder. The *X* would substitute for the number 24. This was done twice to indicate it was not coincidental.

Moreover, a portion of the land would be located in a marsh with a river on the west boundary. This would match the geography surrounding the temple, which God showed unto the prophet Ezekiel in a vision, saying,

But the miry places thereof and the marishes thereof shall not be healed; they shall be given to salt. And by the river upon the bank thereof, on this side and on that side, shall grow all trees for meat, whose leaf shall not fade, neither shall the fruit thereof be consumed: it shall bring forth new fruit according to his months, because their waters they issued out of the sanctuary: and the fruit thereof shall be for meat, and the leaf thereof for medicine. (Ezek. 47:11–12)

There is also a natural ancient lake on the property, which was originally called Horseshoe Lake because of its shape and also to allude to the horses of the apocalypse. The lake would be given a new name in the 1950s. It was called Lake Alaska during the 1950s and 1960s. The name was later changed to Holy Day Lake and pronounced as Holiday Lake. It is the name that it is called today.

The grandparents of Prophet Ellis and their offspring faced many challenges in keeping the property as white landowners sought to swindle them out of it. Most of these were descendants of the Stephen F. Austin's Old Three Hundred or those closely associated with them either by blood or business.

It is perfectly clear that the distribution of land to the twelve tribes, as set out in Ezekiel chapters 47 and 48, does not correspond to the geographical realities of today's Palestine. This is because the temple is to be in the new promised land. This is America. The Lord alluded to this as soon as He began to speak to Ezekiel about His temple in chapter 40 when he showed him the frame of a city. It is the city, which Jesus associated with the hidden candle; a city that sits on a mountain and cannot be hidden. It is a city that is measured and identified by the Key of David. The Bible refers to this key as a measuring line because of its distinct features.

> In the visions of God brought he me into the land of Israel, and set me upon a very high mountain, by which was as the frame of a city on the south. And he brought me thither, and, behold, there was a man, whose appearance was like the appearance of brass, with a line of flax in his hand, and a measuring reed; and he stood in the gate. (Ezek. 40:2–3)

> Ye are the light of the world. A city that is set on an hill cannot be hid. Neither do men light a candle, and put it under a bushel, but on a candlestick; and it giveth light unto all that are in the house. (Matt. 5:14–15)

> And I John saw the holy city, new Jerusalem, coming down from God out of heaven, prepared as a bride adorned for her husband. And I heard a great voice out of heaven saying, Behold, the tabernacle of God is with men, and he will dwell with them, and they shall be his people, and God himself shall be with them, and be their God. And he carried me away in the spirit to a great and high mountain, and shewed me that great city, the holy Jerusalem, descending out of heaven from God. (Rev. 21:2–3, 10)

The Lord makes it clear to Ezekiel in chapter 43 that Old Jerusalem and the promised land have been defiled by centuries of bloodshed and whoredom.

In preparation for this new revelation that God would give to Prophet Ellis, his relatives would build a small sanctuary on this property around the early 1900s. The sanctuary was properly named New Revelation. The original structure was destroyed by the 1932 hurricane, and a new wood frame structure was rebuilt in the same survey but on a different plot of land about two miles further north. It is in use until this day.

David's twenty-four musical elders and their twelve sons each were ordered to do something very strange but also very significant toward today's revelation. They were ordered to prophesy with their instruments. Why is this important? It is because God has raised Shubael up, as one of the greatest musicians of our time. Until his untimely death, he has used his feet to prophesy of the coming of the beast with two horns. These two horns are the two horns on Islam's crescent moon. God ordered Shubael, who represented the whole house of Israel, to put the moon under his feet. A biblical account of this is found in Revelation 12:1.

> And there appeared a great wonder in heaven; a woman clothed with the sun, and the moon under her feet, and upon her head a crown of twelve stars: And she being with child cried, travailing in birth, and pained to be delivered. (Rev. 12:1–2)

God has raised up Shubael as Michael Jackson who would use his feet and music to prophesy of those things to come. The moonwalk, which can only be performed by moving backwards, signified the rise of the Antichrist under Islam and his ultimate defeat by the Lord of Lords and King of Kings. In addition to these, the land has been measured to the exact measurements of the walls given by God unto the prophet Ezekiel.

The latter house of God is to be built by the man who is called the BRANCH. The term *BRANCH* is spelled in all capital letters because of the special attention that this subject warrants. The 3rd, 4th, and 6th chapters of Zechariah show that the stone and the candlesticks are the same.

> And speak unto him, saying, Thus speaketh the Lord of hosts, saying, Behold the man whose name is The Branch; and he shall grow up out of his place, and he shall build the temple of the Lord: Even he shall build the temple of the Lord; and he shall bear the glory, and shall sit and rule upon his throne; and he shall be a priest upon his throne: and the counsel of peace shall be between them both. And they that are far off shall come and build in the temple of the Lord, and ye shall know that the Lord of hosts hath sent me unto you. (Zech. 6:12–13, 15)

The 3rd and 4th chapters of Zechariah tell us just how the Lord will bring the BRANCH about and what shall distinguish him from others. It is the power of the Key of David, which inspired the last words of verse 15 in Zechariah chapter 6 above. It says that, "Ye shall know that the LORD of hosts hath sent me unto you." The BRANCH shall come forth with the stone that was laid before Joshua and engraved by God.

> Hear now, O Joshua the high priest, thou, and thy fellows that sit before thee: for they are men wondered at: for, behold, I will bring forth my servant the Branch. For behold the stone that I have laid before Joshua; upon one stone shall be seven eyes: behold, I will engrave the graving thereof, saith the Lord of hosts, and I will remove the iniquity of that land in one day. (Zech. 3:8–9)

After this, Zechariah is shown a vision of the seven golden candlesticks and the great mountain from which this stone was cut without hands.

Chapter 4 of Zechariah begins with the conjunction *and*. This shows that chapter 4 is essentially a continuation of chapter 3, where God promised to bring forth the BRANCH with the stone laid before Joshua.

> And the angel that talked with me came again, and waked me, as a man that is wakened out of his sleep. And said unto me, What seest thou? And I said, I have looked, and behold a candlestick all of gold, with a bowl upon the top of it, and his seven lamps thereon, and seven pipes to the seven lamps, which are upon the top thereof: And two olive trees by it, one upon the right side of the bowl, and the other upon the left side thereof. So I answered and spake to the angel that talked with me, saying, What are these, my lord? Then the angel that talked with me answered and said unto me, Knowest thou not what these be? And I said, No, my lord. Then he answered and spake unto me, saying, This is the word of the Lord unto Zerubbabel, saying, Not by might, nor by power, but by my spirit, saith the Lord of hosts.
>
> Who art thou, O great mountain? before Zerubbabel thou shalt become a plain: and he shall bring forth the headstone thereof with shoutings, crying, Grace, grace unto it. (Zech. 4:1–7)

This headstone or cornerstone, which is brought forth by the BRANCH, is the stone mentioned in chapter 3 verse 8–9, which is the stone laid before Joshua upon which are seven eyes. This keystone unlocks the door to one of the earth's most golden secrets, which is alluded to when the olive branches empties the golden oil out of themselves. This is just one of many reasons why the Key of David cannot be debunked by the opposition. This key opens the door to reveal the hidden mysteries of oil and gas.

Notes

REFERENCES: www.sontoglory.com Millennial Temple Model of Ezekiel's vision, Third 3d. Chapter 7. The millennial Temple "Describe the temple to the house of Israel, that they may be ashamed...

www.middletownbiblechurch.com The Millennial Temple – Ezekiel 40-48. The Millennial Temple of Ezekiel 40-48 (An exercise in Literal Interpretation) Dr. John C. Whitecomb...

www.niblewatchman.com The Millennial Temple – Bible Watchman

The Millennial Temple "In the visions of God brought he me into the land of Israel, and set me upon a...

www.gracethrufaith.com/ask-abible-teacher/...

Why Sacrifice Animals In The Millennium? What would be the need or purpose of animal sacrifices still being offered up in the Millennium.

https//www.ids.org/topics/millennium? Ian...

The Millennium—Church of Jesus Christ of Latter Day Saints

When LDS members speak of the Millennium, they refer to the 1,000 years following Jesus' Second...

searchinsany.hubpages.com...

Why Did Jesus Never Mention the Millennium Temple?

Many believe Ezekiel's Temple will be built in the near future, complete with animal sacrifices, the...

www.keithhunt.com/milemp.html

The Millennium Temple?

Several old testament prophets predicted that during the millennium, Israel believers...

Shubael Marsh (The Handbook of Texas Online State

www.tshaonline.org/handbook/online/articl...

Shubael Marsh (1801-1868) Shubael Marsh was one of Stephen F. Austin's Old Three Hundred colonists, was born...

Chapter 18

Prophet Ellis Is Certified as a Prophet by a Historical Record

The messianic message is of such importance for both the churches and world governments, thus, it is vital that God's messenger be certified as a prophet. Such certification must be in accordance with the protocol given by God to Moses in the 18th chapter of Deuteronomy. God promised to raise up a prophet like unto Moses. God told Moses that He would put His words in this prophet's mouth, and whosoever will not hearken unto God's words, which this prophet speaks in God's name, that God will require it of him. Would God, therefore, send a messenger who could not be certified as the two candlesticks? The answer is *no*. Here are the words for the protocol of a prophet recorded in chapter 18 verses 18 through 22 of Deuteronomy by Moses.

> I will raise them up a Prophet from among their brethren, like unto thee, and will put my words in his mouth; and he shall speak unto them all that I shall command him. And it shall come to pass, that whosoever will not hearken unto my words which he shall speak in my name, I will require it of him.
>
> But the prophet, which shall presume to speak a word in my name, which I have not commanded him to speak, or that shall speak in the name of other gods, even that prophet shall die. And if thou say in thine heart, How shall we know the word which the LORD hath not spoken?
>
> When a prophet speaketh in the name of the LORD, if the thing follow not, nor come to pass, that is the thing which the LORD hath not spoken, but the prophet hath spoken it presumptuously: thou shalt not be afraid of him. (Deut. 18:18–22)

In God's continued dialogue to Moses concerning His prophet, God recognized the role that racism would play in His people, hearing or forbearing God's word via His messenger. Therefore, God spoke to racism.

Miriam and Aaron, the sister and brother of Moses, had spoken against Moses because of the black woman whom God had given Moses for a wife. It was an Ethiopian woman of the Negro race. Their conduct angered God to the extent that God spit in the face of Miriam turning her snow white. It cannot be determined from the scripture if spit is used as a metaphor or if it actually was spit from God's mouth. We will assume that a metaphor is used here; however, the end result is nevertheless the same. What is certain is that it is intended to address the issues of today in the churches and those already being encountered by God's messenger.

> And Miriam and Aaron spake against Moses because of the Ethiopian woman whom he had married: for he had married an Ethiopian woman. And they said, Hath the LORD indeed spoken only by Moses? hath he not spoken also by us? And the LORD heard it. (Now the man Moses was very meek, above all the men which were upon the face of the earth.)
>
> And the LORD spake suddenly unto Moses, and unto Aaron, and unto Miriam, Come out ye three unto the tabernacle of the congregation. And they three came out. And the LORD came down in the pillar of the cloud, and stood in the door of the tabernacle, and called Aaron and Miriam: and they both came forth.
>
> And he said, Hear now my words: If there be a prophet among you, I the LORD will make myself known unto him in a vision, and will speak unto him in a dream. My servant Moses is not so, who is

faithful in all mine house. With him will I speak mouth to mouth, even apparently, and not in dark speeches; and the similitude of the Lord shall he behold: wherefore then were ye not afraid to speak against my servant Moses? And the anger of the Lord was kindled against them; and he departed.

And the cloud departed from off the tabernacle; and, behold, Miriam became leprous, white as snow: and Aaron looked upon Miriam, and, behold, she was leprous. And Aaron said unto Moses, Alas, my lord, I beseech thee, lay not the sin upon us, wherein we have done foolishly, and wherein we have sinned. Let her not be as one dead, of whom the flesh is half consumed when he cometh out of his mother's womb.

And Moses cried unto the Lord, saying, Heal her now, O God, I beseech thee. And the Lord said unto Moses, If her father had but spit in her face, should she not be ashamed seven days? let her be shut out from the camp seven days, and after that let her be received in again. And Miriam was shut out from the camp seven days: and the people journeyed not till Miriam was brought in again. (Num. 12:1–15)

I will defend Prophet Ellis as being a proven and certified prophet of God by showing that he have met God's established protocol for a prophet. It is relevant that some of the things that he has spoken prophetically were recorded in advance and have thus come to pass. It is also relevant that such prophesies are the substance of biblical things prophesied to come to pass. These things would also alter and change the directions of world governments.

A diary must be kept of the divine messages as they were received from the Most High God. God has promised that He would make himself known to His prophet in a vision and speak unto him in a dream. I was given access to Prophet Ellis's voluminous dream diary, which began in April 1998 and has continued until this day. Each entry has the date of the dream, the time, and the subject. Many appear to have been divinely coded by date. For example: the coming of the 9/11 terror attacks on the World Trade Center was recorded on September 11, 1999. It was two years before.

The devastating 9.0 magnitude earthquake, which caused the historic tsunami in Japan on March 11, 2011, was recorded in a four-part dream on April 25, 2005, beginning at 2:50 a.m. and ending at approximately 5:30 a.m. When Prophet Ellis prayed for an interpretation of the dream, the Lord responded, saying, "I will give you one." He then said the tsunami is Magog. Prophet Ellis then wrote in parenthesis (Russia) assuming that Magog was Russia. However, a few minutes later, he enters another dream where God shows him a train, which he called the "train of death." His diary records that he gets out of bed and turns on the news channel and learns of a massive train wreck in Japan. It would be almost exactly six years before this earthquake-triggered tsunami arrive as a train of death in Japan.

There are hundreds of others who are of a historical nature that has either come to pass, yet to come, or those that are now. Among those that are now involved is the administration of Russia's Vladimir Putin. I will use the prophesy on Vladimir Putin to illustrate how Prophet Ellis can be called a certified prophet. *Certified* means to declare something is true or correct by an official spoken, written, or printed statement.

On December 8, 1999, while Boris Yeltsin was still governing as president of Russia, no western intelligence or foreign intelligence was aware that a coup d'état was imminent in Moscow's Red Square. Yet on this 8th day of December 1999, Prophet Ellis would prepare a prophetic warning to the US government that was certified by a US district clerk for the Southern District of Texas at Houston. His 8th chapter motion, containing more than sixty pages, warned of a new and malevolent leader who rise to power on or before January 1, 2000. On January 1, 2000, Russia's Boris Yeltsin was ousted, and Vladimir Putin was in as prophesied.

Prophet Ellis's prophesies were made a part of a habeas corpus petition that was certified by US district clerk, Michael M. Milby for the Southern District of Texas Houston Division, under

Cause Number H 99-4239. This prophesy was just one of several. It is not necessary to list any more than three certified major prophesies that have come to pass and thus have changed the course of many world governments. These follow the protocol that was given by God. Thus, it is not possible for these to be debunked by a strong opposition. These are just some of the words extracted from Prophet Ellis's petition to the court. They began on page two of the petition, saying as follows:

> This petitioner will show the court that the facts of his petition are rooted in seven years of research and investigations. That his petition is extracted from more than seven (7) years, and sixteen volumes of assiduous and painstaking work. That petitioner's work carried him to several eastern and western European countries, including Russia. And the culmination of this work has lead petitioner to determine and inform this court as follows:

> This petitioner will show the court through his testimony and from the court's careful examination of the facts of this petition—"the existence of a coalition of international white supremacists: these includes factions of clansmen, skinheads, neo-Nazi, the World Church, and Wiccan worshipers at US military facilities, who are planning an imminent coup d'etat. These have piggybacked with communist Russians to seize world power on or before January 1, 2000.

> The petitioner will show that this malevolent consortium has remained invisible until the filing of this petition. It is this invisibility that prompted the self-confidence Empire to reference itself, as the invisible empire of the KKK.

Prophet Ellis was unaware that the white triangular stone on Marlboro cigarette packets, coupled with other symbols, were complex Masonic symbols for the Key of David. It is a key to be revealed by the Branch of David, whom God has called the BRANCH. He is the messianic messenger referred to biblically as the two candlesticks and the two olive branches (Rev. 11:1–19). Prophet Ellis arrived back in the United States during the morning of April 19, 1993, to break the Marlboro cigarette story. He had only heard of the Branch Davidians and David Koresh a few days before, from one of his part-time student journalist attending Moscow State University. The student simply told him that David Koresh and some of his followers were in a bloody standoff with federal law enforcement officers.

Arriving at Houston Intercontinental Airport, he drove to his home in Missouri City, Texas, with one thing on his mind. This was getting to the press for his Marlboro cigarette story. However, when he turned on his television set, before he could put away his luggage from his Moscow trip, the story mentioned to him about David Koresh was playing out live on local and national television sets. What caught his attention was David Koresh had sent word out by his attorney, Dick DeGuerin, that he would surrender after opening the seven seals. Three he said he had already opened and he had only four more to go. Little did Prophet Ellis know was these are the seals that are opened by the Key of David. Yet Prophet Ellis could not recall having heard of the seven seals. Therefore, he was curious about just what are these Seven Seals. The government, to whom he was negotiating Koresh's surrender, knew that these were the national seals of the United States and its G7 partners. They would not take a chance on whether or not he was going to open them. They could not afford the risk. Prophet Ellis watched in disbelief, as the compound seemed to have turned to fire, smoke, and ash with the body of the false messiah. Therefore, the habeas corpus petition continued to warn of those things to come on January 1, 2000, as follows:

> Petitioner will show the court that this invisible empire knew that their existence would one day be revealed by the prophetic branch of David, "the second Messiah." (See References section 5, p.1.) In their futile attempt to circumvent such revelation, petitioner will show the court that this empire organized the Branch Davidian cult at Waco. Petitioner would show that their organizing of the cult was part of a larger scheme with broad and apocalyptic consequences. That it was aimed at deceiving the world and usher in a malevolent Russian king on or about January 1, 2000.

Petitioner will show that such plan is still in place. That the empire is attempting to deceive the world with a false Christ out of Russia. And that David Koresh was held out as the messenger (branch of David) to warn and announce the second coming of Christ.

The certification of this historical event in many parts were being spiritually guided without Prophet Ellis's conscious awareness. This is how the spirit works with the prophet knowing only in part. This subtle working of the Holy Spirit is confirmed by the apostle Paul in one of his letters to the church at Corinth. Paul writes as follows, saying:

> For we know in part, and we prophesy in part. But when that which is perfect is come, then that which is in part shall be done away. (1 Cor. 13:9–10)

We are able to confirm the certification of three of Prophet Ellis's historical prophesies: the coming of the 9/11 terror attacks recorded on September 11, 1999, the coming of the March 1, 2011, Japan 9.0 earthquake and tsunami that was recorded in four parts on April 25, 2005, and rise of Vladimir Putin precisely on January 1, 2000, in Russia.

In Revelation 11:6, God promises to give power to His two witnesses to shut heaven, that it rain not in the days of their prophesy, and He will give them power over waters to turn them to blood and to smite the earth with all plagues. In volume 125 of Prophet Ellis's prophetic library, which is dated October 28, 2011, he warned of the historic droughts now faced by California and other states. This certified prophesy was sent to our last two presidents, secretaries of state, Texas governor Rick Perry, and Pastor John Hagee among others. It warned of the consequences for ignoring the call to build the Lord's house. Although the public may be unaware, Hurricane Katrina, Hurricane Sandy, and other unnatural weather systems stem from the power that God has given unto His two witnesses to complete their assignment.

God knew that if He sent forth His two witnesses clothed in sackcloth that they would be rejected by racial bigots within and outside of the churches. Sackcloth is a biblical metaphor used as a Bible code to describe the ethnicity of God's two witnesses who are black. Sackcloth was a black garment worn in time of mourning by the ancients.

> And I beheld when he had opened the sixth seal, and, lo, there was a great earthquake; and the sun became black as sackcloth of hair, and the moon became as blood. (Rev. 6:12)

> And I will give power unto my two witnesses, and they shall prophesy a thousand two hundred and threescore days, clothed in sackcloth. (Rev. 11:3)

> Look not upon me, because I am black, because the sun hath looked upon me: my mother's children were angry with me; they made me the keeper of the vineyards; but mine own vineyard have I not kept. (Song of Sol. 1:6)

> And there appeared a great wonder in heaven; a woman clothed with the sun, and the moon under her feet, and upon her head a crown of twelve stars. (Rev. 12:1)

Volume number 9 dated April 22, 1998, and November 10, 1998, of Ellis's library is a certified record where God had him to prophesy against Special Prosecutor Kenneth Starr to save President Clinton from removal from office by impeachment. The prophesies were sent to Special Counsel Starr, Attorney Bob Bennett, President Bill Clinton, and US District Judge Norma Holloway Johnson, informing the prosecutor that he had been sent to fight against him with the rod of his mouth. Ellis showed that the president's ordeal was a divine act for a special sign for these trouble times.

The special prosecutor considered the prophesies a threat and contacted the Austin, Texas, bureau office of the FBI to arrest Prophet Ellis. FBI Special Agent Sykes Houston took the warrant but returned it back to Kenneth Starr when he realized that Starr's office was sending him into a situation of a divine nature. Starr became frustrated in his inability to prevail against both Ellis and Clinton and resigned as special prosecutor.

The Marlboro graphics are included to show how God revealed this stone to Prophet Ellis systematically over a period of more than twenty years, without Prophet Ellis having any knowledge thereof. On the left (see following page) is the cover of his 1993 spring issue of his *Moscow Business Journal*. The article itself is not included in my thesis. His headline is: "Marlboro Man Busted! Secret Code Cracked!" His titled shook the conscious of Phillip Morris's management, and they cancelled a scheduled interview. As Freemasons, Phillip Morris was aware, and Ellis had no knowledge that God was about to give him the white stone appearing symbolically on Marlboro brands.

Fifteen years after the Marlboro article and the election of America's first African American president of Hebrew stock, the Phillip Morris company would introduce a new symbolic message called "Black." These words would be written across the white stone to signal that this white stone has now become a black stone. Ellis is a certified prophet.

Notes

REFERENCES: Verification for the fulfillment of Prophesies was obtained from the archives of The United States District Court Memorandum certified by District Clerk Michel N. Milby on February 1, 2000 under Civil Action H-00-4239. The Court's Memorandum preserved in both its archives, and the Prophetic Library of Prophet Ellis, provides a summary of Prophet Ellis' prophesy. Although the Court had an opportunity to confirm the fulfillment of his central prophesy which predicted a New Russian Leader on or before January 1, 2000, the Court chose instead to omit this significant truth from its finding. Collectively however, the global archives of all major news organizations, taken with Prophet Ellis' Court filing, and the Court subsequent ruling, works jointly to certify this profound prophesy which changed the world forever.

OTHER RESOURCES AND ARCHIVES: The Imperial House of Russia. House of Romanovs. The Habeas Corus case in the United States District Court stems from a mystery which shrouds a diabolical mechanism to circumvent Prophet Ellis' Mission to Russia after the fall of the Soviet Union. It was orchestrated by Alexander Romanov, a Russian National with an American residence. In 1983 he infiltrates Prophet Ellis' Houston Real Estate business and become a limited partner in a partnership that went bust in a faltering economy. Prophet Ellis had no conscious awareness that GOD had chosen him for a special end-time mission. Based on revelation now coming to mind, Satan knew his mission, and its threat to his world kingdoms. (Revelation 11:19) The Romanovs', who received this stone, and the power of it, after the fall of the East Roman Empire, had ruled Russia for more than 300 years until the October Revolution of 1917. It is the same stone which Satan challenge Jesus to turn to bread if he is indeed the Son of God. (Matthew 4:1-10)

After the partnership went bust, Romanov would bring a frivolous charge against Ellis for the small investment he had lost. An indictment against Ellis would be handed down by a Harris County Grand Jury on October 4, 1984, based on Romanov's complaint. Trial would begin on March 3, 1986. In an effort to hide Romanov, his case #411777 would be dropped; but Ellis would be convicted on five others. On May 18, 1988, all of Ellis' appeals had been exhausted in what he described to the FBI as a master chess game of judicial fraud. The FBI took charge of the complaint, and silence would prevail on all sides for more than another eight years while Ellis remained free. His Russian mission would not be circumvented.

On May 18, 1988, the LORD appeared to Ellis and informed him to seal up a prophesy that GOD would give him, and have it remain sealed. GOD had him to mail a registered letter to himself with a sealed prophesy. This was after all Court appeals had been exhausted, and a mandate for Ellis' arrest was imminent. Ellis did not know the reasons for this prophesy; which has remained sealed until the date of this thesis. GOD instructed him to write in the Prophesy that he would not be going to prison for a very long time; and ask himself, how could he know such in advance? Ellis was unaware that this was the voice of the LORD until many years later. Ellis mission to Russia would be completed eight years later on Aril 19, 1994. When Ellis arrived back from Moscow at his Missouri City, Texas home, the local sheriff was waiting at the direction of a hidden enemy.

ADDITIONAL RESOURCES: The Mysteries of The Unknown By the Editors of Time-Life Books Copyright 1987: Time-Life editors chronicles the mysteries of Cleopatra's Needles describing how they were coveted by the Romans. During the 15th Century the Roman Catholic Church had a similar Egyptian Needle that was moved from Egypt to St. Peter's Square where it remains standing until this day. The Editors of Time-Life writes the following about Cleopatra's Needles:

Egypt's stone obelisks—originally raised in homage to the sun—gods—have been coveted since Roman times as symbols of conquest and mysterious power. Weighing an average of 150 tons, the granite pillars challenged those who would carry them off, as Sir James Alexander discovered in 1877.

The obelisk of the Englishman's attentions was Cleopatra's Needle, Sixty-eight feet tall. It had been presented to England half a century earlier by the Egyptian ruler Muhammad Ali. Attempts to collect the prize in Alexander, however, had met only with frustration.

Other Sources: The United States Postal Service official records and seal for Registered Mail Number R 307 176 205 for the sealed prophesy entered more than a quarter century ago which has remained locked, and sealed. (See graphic below)

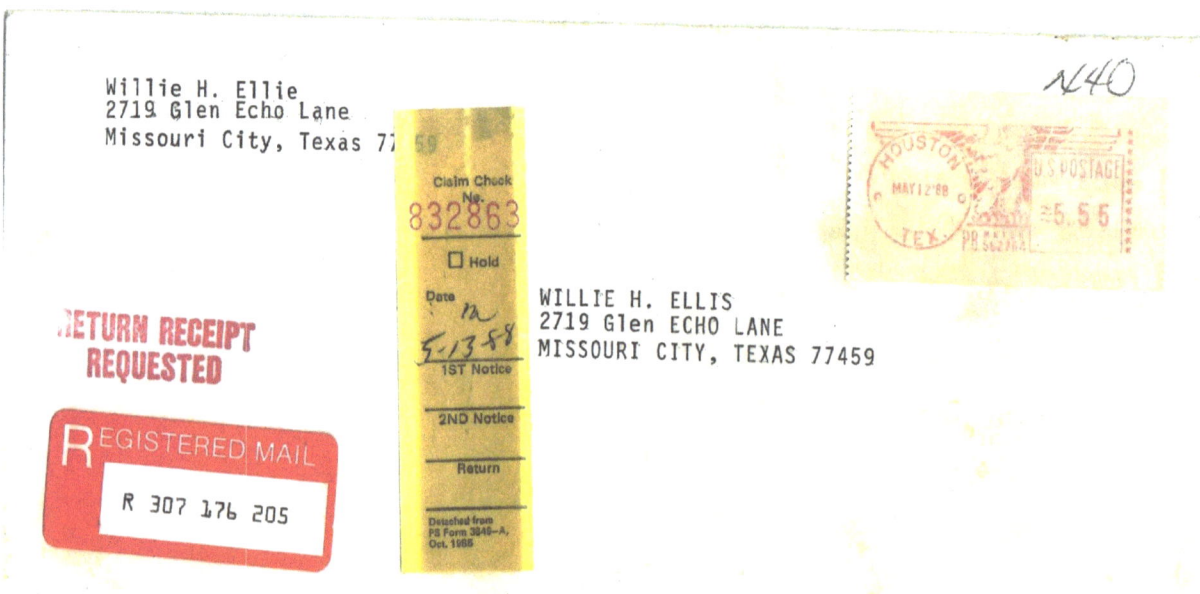

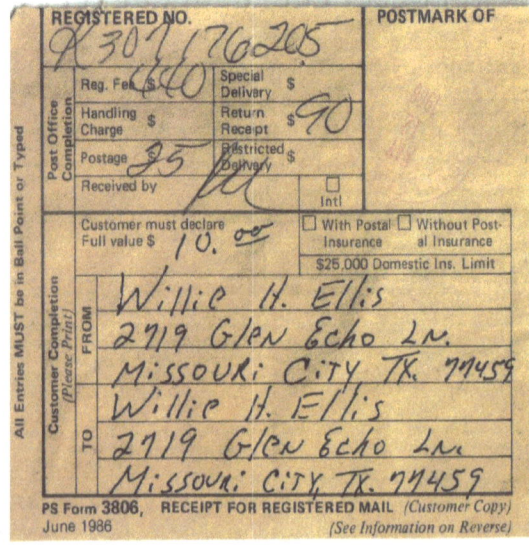

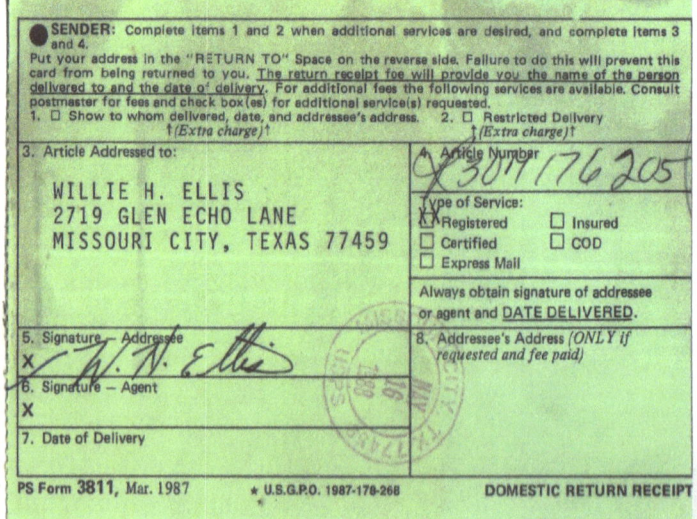

Chapter 19

Confirming Cleopatra's Needles as ISIS Two Horns

Once a man is certified a messenger of God, it would not only be foolish not to listen to him but also it would be dangerous, especially if he is known to be a prophet but is rejected for bias reasons such as race and envy. It must be carefully noted that God knew race, and religious bias would be key factors as to whether His end-time messenger would be accepted or rejected. Therefore, those final words of the Old Testament end with this prophetic warning from God through His prophet Malachi, which says:

> Behold, I will send you Elijah the prophet before the coming of the great and dreadful day of the Lord: And he shall turn the heart of the fathers to the children, and the heart of the children to their fathers, lest I come and smite the earth with a curse. (Mal. 4:5–6)

> I will raise them up a Prophet from among their brethren, like unto thee, and will put my words in his mouth; and he shall speak unto them all that I shall command him. And it shall come to pass, that whosoever will not hearken unto my words which he shall speak in my name, I will require it of him. (Deut. 18:18–19)

Now that a United States federal court has unknowingly and unwittingly certified Prophet Ellis as God's two candlesticks and two olive branch witnesses, Prophet Ellis will reveal the mystery of the two candlesticks. His revelation of the two candlesticks is original, convincing, and conclusive. Moreover, their identities are confirmed by clear, simple, and verifiable historical and biblical facts.

The two candlesticks are the substance of the great stones that God hid at the entry to Pharaoh's house in Egypt. He would have the prophet Jeremiah to symbolically hide stones, which God had already hidden. These stones would be a precision cut obelisk shaped as two candlesticks.

I shall argue and thereafter prove that the stones, known as Cleopatra's Needles, once stood at the entry to Pharaoh's house in Egypt. Proving this is critical because it is where the Bible records that the stones were hidden. However, how can you hide something if it is published openly in the Bible? It was God's plan to publish in the Scripture where the stones were hidden so that His adversary would move them so that God's messenger would not be able to find them based on where the Scripture says they were hidden. Yet God never said he hid them at the entry to Pharaoh's house. He only instructed Jeremiah to do so, after His instructions, God then told Jeremiah that He would set Nebuchadnezzar's throne upon these stones that He had hidden.

> So they came into the land of Egypt: for they obeyed not the voice of the Lord: thus came they even to Tahpanhes. Then came the word of the Lord unto Jeremiah in Tahpanhes, saying, Take great stones in thine hand, and hide them in the clay in the brickkiln, which is at the entry of Pharaoh's house in Tahpanhes, in the sight of the men of Judah; And say unto them, Thus saith the Lord of hosts, the God of Israel; Behold, I will send and take Nebuchadrezzar the king of Babylon, my servant, and will set his throne upon these stones that I have hid; and he shall spread his royal pavilion over them. (Jer. 43:7–10)

These great stones were raised as two pillars shaped as two candlesticks. They represented the power and authority that God himself had given to Pharaoh. When Daniel was interpreting Nebuchadnezzar's dream regarding the secret of this stone, Daniel said in verse 21 of chapter 2, "God removeth kings, and setteth up kings." These Egyptian pillars represent the authority given by God unto Pharaoh. The two horns worn on the Egyptian sun goddess Isis's crown are symbols for these two pillars.

Egyptian history and antiquities confirm that Egyptians worshipped Queen Cleopatra as the resurrected Egyptian sun goddess Isis. Egyptian coins also depict Cleopatra as Isis. In addition, my research and investigation has confirmed that Cleopatra's biography, written by Joyce Tyldesley, also confirms Cleopatra is believed to be the resurrected sun goddess Isis. Therefore, Prophet Ellis has correctly identified Cleopatra's Needles as ISIS Needles represented by her crown with two horns and a sundial between them. These two horns are the horns of the beast known as the Antichrist in Revelation 13:18. It is the beast that is raised from the bottomless pit and kills God's two witnesses, who identify him in the street of that city that is spiritually called Sodom and Egypt. Here are the supporting scriptures provided by Prophet Ellis from his prophetic library.

> And I beheld another beast coming up out of the earth; and he had two horns like a lamb, and he spake as a dragon. And he exerciseth all the power of the first beast before him, and causeth the earth and them which dwell therein to worship the first beast, whose deadly wound was healed. And he had power to give life unto the image of the beast, that the image of the beast should both speak, and cause that as many as would not worship the image of the beast should be killed. (Rev. 13:11–12, 15)

> And I saw thrones, and they sat upon them, and judgment was given unto them: and I saw the souls of them that were beheaded for the witness of Jesus, and for the word of God, and which had not worshipped the beast, neither his image, neither had received his mark upon their foreheads, or in their hands; and they lived and reigned with Christ a thousand years. (Rev. 20:4)

NOTE: this is the beheading now being perpetrated upon Christians by ISIS so-called terrorist army in Syria.

Cleopatra Needles, which we will now refer to as ISIS Needles, were moved to the banks of London's River Thames in 1877, and its twin was moved to New York Central Park in 1880. After receiving these two Egyptian candlesticks stone pillars, New York City and London then became the cities that are spiritually called Sodom and Egypt, where God's two candlestick witnesses are killed by the resurrected beast with two horns.

> And I will give power unto my two witnesses, and they shall prophesy a thousand two hundred and threescore days, clothed in sackcloth. These are the two olive trees, and the two candlesticks standing before the God of the earth. And if any man will hurt them, fire proceedeth out of their mouth, and devoureth their enemies: and if any man will hurt them, he must in this manner be killed.

> These have power to shut heaven, that it rain not in the days of their prophecy: and have power over waters to turn them to blood, and to smite the earth with all plagues, as often as they will. And when they shall have finished their testimony, the beast that ascendeth out of the bottomless pit shall make war against them, and shall overcome them, and kill them.

> And their dead bodies shall lie in the street of the great city, which spiritually is called Sodom and Egypt, where also our Lord was crucified. And they of the people and kindreds and tongues and nations shall see their dead bodies three days and an half, and shall not suffer their dead bodies to be put in graves. And they that dwell upon the earth shall rejoice over them, and make merry, and shall send gifts one to another; because these two prophets tormented them that dwelt on the earth. And after three days and an half the spirit of life from God entered into them, and they stood upon their feet; and great fear fell upon them which saw them. And they heard a great voice from heaven saying

unto them, Come up hither. And they ascended up to heaven in a cloud; and their enemies beheld them. And the same hour was there a great earthquake, and the tenth part of the city fell, and in the earthquake were slain of men seven thousand: and the remnant were affrighted, and gave glory to the God of heaven. The second woe is past; and, behold, the third woe cometh quickly.

And the seventh angel sounded; and there were great voices in heaven, saying, The kingdoms of this world are become the kingdoms of our Lord, and of his Christ; and he shall reign for ever and ever. And the four and twenty elders, which sat before God on their seats, fell upon their faces, and worshipped God, Saying, We give thee thanks, O Lord God Almighty, which art, and wast, and art to come; because thou hast taken to thee thy great power, and hast reigned.

And the nations were angry, and thy wrath is come, and the time of the dead, that they should be judged, and that thou shouldest give reward unto thy servants the prophets, and to the saints, and them that fear thy name, small and great; and shouldest destroy them which destroy the earth.

And the temple of God was opened in heaven, and there was seen in his temple the ark of his testament: and there were lightnings, and voices, and thunderings, and an earthquake, and great hail. (Rev. 11:3–19)

The foregoing scripture shows that both the people and the nations shall have wholesale contempt and hatred for God's messenger. They shall rejoice over their deaths and leave their bodies lying in the streets. They will treat them no better than they treated Jesus whose own people turned him over to the Romans for execution by a cruel crucifixion.

One Candlestick Stands in New York Central Park

In the spring of 1993, it being the same time, Prophet Ellis returned from Moscow, Russia, to publish the Marlboro cigarette story. Also, in the spring of 1993, the New York Metropolitan Museum of Art was publishing *The New York Obelisk* or *How Cleopatra's Needle Came To New York and What Happened When It Got Here*. I have verified this from the copyright date printed in both publications. It would be more than twelve years before Prophet Ellis be introduced to what is called Cleopatra's Needles. These came as a gift from Ismail and Tewfik Pasha, who were Egyptian Khedive and maternal brothers. They were also Islamic Freemasons called Shriners. Their gifts were a clever move aimed at perpetrating a diabolical act. Their aim was to hide these two candlesticks from God's two witnesses.

Notes

REFERENCES: The Daily Graphic (July 30, 1880). The announcement of Egypt's gift caused great excitement in New York in a cartoonist's vision in the Daily Graphic; a would be welcoming committee includes William H. Vanderbilt and William Henry Hurlbert, holding a copy of his paper, the New York World. Hurlbert took credit for suggesting the gift to the Khedive.

Harper's Weekly, July 3, 1889. Ismail Pasha (1830–1895). At the opening of the Suez Canal, the Khedive told Hurlbert that "he had been struck by the absence of the American flag from the great parade of ships of all nations through the Suez Canal and he was firmly convinced that the prosperity of Egypt would be advanced by…whatever he could do to bring Egypt and America more closely together". Cleopatra's Needle made an impressive token of friendship.

New York Herald, November 3, 1879: Fawfig Pasha (1852–1892). "There has been all sort of pressure upon me to retain the obelisk," the prince told a newspaper reporter. "But I assure you it will give me great pleasure to hear of this obelisk being erected in America, where, I hope, it will not only create interest there in the ancient Egyptian monuments, but, by awakening general inquiry as to Egypt, may possibly lead to the establishment of trade between the United States and Egypt."

Evening Telegram, November 6, 1879. Not all Americans were thrilled by Egypt's gift. "A petition remonstrating against the removal of Cleopatra's Needle is being circulated and has received numerous influential signatures." The new York Sun (October 31, 1879) joined the opposition and labeled the obelisk "terrific humbug". It has no beauty and no shapeliness. It is only a broken, decayed and disfigured old block of stone." Such carping was soon lost in the swell of enthusiasm for the impending arrival of Cleopatra's Needle.

The New York Herald, November 1, 1879: The obelisk with scaffolding in place. The New York Herald reported that "The gallant Commander Gorringe shows himself alive to his duties as an American Naval Officer. He has hoisted the American flag over the granite column…and threatens to shoot on the spot any sacrilegious creditor who proposes to haul it down. In other words, the obelisk is now surrounded with a blaze of glory, and Commander Gorringe the central figure in defending the flag. This is an inspiring spectacle.

The New York Obelisk, (p. 42) On October 10, 1880, a parade of nine thousand Freemasons marched up Fifth Avenue, bands blaring, to Graywacke Knoll for a grand and solemn cornerstone ceremony. Preparing to lower the cornerstone, October 10, 1880. For the Freemasons the cube of polished marble that had been found under the pedestal was thought to represent one of their most significant symbols, the Perfect Ashlar.

Chapter 20

The Statue of Liberty: Her Seven Spikes Opens a Golden Door

WORLD BOOK ILLUSTRATIONS BY BIRNEY LETTICK

Cleopatra's Needles, the Washington Memorial, and the Statue of Liberty—all bare the Freemasonry cornerstone symbolizing that they are all the works of Freemasonry. These three monuments work individually and collectively to confirm the mystery of God's seal in the earth, and they also confirm two of the greatest mysteries in the Bible. These two mysteries are God's deliverance of Israel from Egyptian slavery and His raising of His Son Jesus from the dead.

The image of the Washington Memorial in chapter 3 can be found in all Freemasonry Bibles. It contains a golden riddle that is written in cursive in the last sentence. It is a dark sentence that alludes to a close relationship between the symbolism hidden on the Liberty and the Washington Memorial. This last sentence is Freemasonry's description of what the Washington Memorial looks like. They write this golden riddle to describe Liberty whose proper name is Liberty Enlightening the World. The sentence reads, "It looks like a giant spike which God had driven, saying, 'Now stake a claim for the home of Liberty.'" The term *spike* was used to allude to the seven spikes in Liberty's crown, which conceals a golden secret regarding the seven golden candlesticks that are concealed in the Washington Memorial. The seven spikes in Liberty's crown are actually seven miniature Washington Memorials. These spikes are designed to be rays from the rising sun. Liberty is the sun goddess Isis, who is rising from the east facing west. It is the Eastern Star of Freemasonry.

There is a poem written by Emma Lazarus and inscribed in Liberty's pedestal that is entitled *The New Colossus*. Liberty was designed after the Colossus of Rhodes. The Colossus of Rhodes was one of the original Seven Wonders of the World. It was built to honor the sun god Helios. Many people do not realize that our sun is actually a star, which rises in the east.

If we are to understand and drink deep from the flowing stream of knowledge of Liberty's symbolism, then we must begin with the poem inscribed in her pedestal. It is the last sentence of that poem that is holding a key that opens a golden door. It is the door to the United States Great Seal.

The New Colossus

Not like the brazen giant of Greek fame,

With conquering limbs astride from land to land;

Here at our sea-washed, sunset gates shall stand

A mighty woman with a torch, whose flame

Is the imprisoned lightning, and her name

Mother of Exiles. From her beacon-hand

Glows world-wide welcome; her mild eyes command.

The air-bridged harbor that twin cities frame.

"Keep, ancient lands, your storied pomp!" cries she

With silent lips. "Give me your tired, your poor,

Your huddled masses yearning to breathe free,

The wretched refuse of your teeming shore.

Send these, the homeless, tempest-tost to me,

I lift my lamp beside the golden door!"

Her lamp is lifted up near her crown, having seven spikes representing the seven golden candlesticks hidden in the Washington Memorial. These are the golden door, which is opened by the Key of David. This key is held symbolically in the left hand of Liberty on the tablet of the Declaration of Independence. This key is the stone known as Cleopatra's Needles hidden in New York Central Park and is duplicated symbolically as the spikes in Liberty's crown. The tablet in her left hand is inscribed with the date of the Declaration of Independence in Roman numerals. It reads July IV, MDCCLXXVI, or July 4, 1776. Pennsylvania is nicknamed the Keystone State.

The poem challenges the intellect of the brightest of the brightest. The poem presents Liberty as the sun by saying, "Her flame is the imprisoned lighting and her name." Her proper name is Liberty Enlightening the World. It is the sun that enlightens the world. The poem title *The New Colossus* confirms her as being the rising sun and the Eastern Star of Masonry.

Rhode Island takes its name and the symbolism of its flag from the Colossus. The Colossus of Rhodes stood in the island of Rhodes in the Mediterranean. It was on the Greek island of Patmos where the prophet John was imprisoned by the Romans when God showed him the Colossus of Rhodes rising up from the sea as the Antichrist with ten horns. These ten horns are kings in the earth. They are represented as ten stars on Rhode Island's state flag. Three of the thirteen golden stars are hidden so that only ten are visible.

The State Flag

The State Bird
Rhode Island Red

    The Keystone in Liberty's left hand is called the Stone of Hope. It is the symbolism of the anchor on Rhode Island's state flag. As stated earlier and confirmed by historical records, the Colossus of Rhodes was built to honor the sun god Helios. A crowing rooster, which is the state bird of Rhode Island, is symbolic of the rising sun. A rooster normally crows at the rising of the sun. He is the biblical symbol of betrayal like the Eastern Star.

> Jesus said unto him, Verily I say unto thee, That this night, before the cock crow, thou shalt deny me thrice. (Matt. 26:34)

Rhode Island gained fame for their love of personal liberty. The state flag, which bares the symbolism of the Stone of Hope, was adopted in 1877, which was the same year this stone was moved from Egypt to the banks of London's River Thames.

    Rhode Island's flag is cleverly crafted to symbolize the two beast of Revelation. One beast has ten horns, and the other has two horns. These are the two beasts described as the Antichrist in Revelation chapter 13. These horns represent the power, which God has given unto the leading nations by these twelve stones hidden in the Washington Memorial. Ten horns plus two horns are equal to twelve horns for the twelve stones and twelve stars. These represent the power of Israel that was given to the gentiles.

WORLD BOOK ILLUSTRATIONS BY BIRNEY LETTICK

And I stood upon the sand of the sea, and saw a beast rise up out of the sea, having seven heads and ten horns, and upon his horns ten crowns, and upon his heads the name of blasphemy.

And I beheld another beast coming up out of the earth; and he had two horns like a lamb, and he spake as a dragon.

And he exerciseth all the power of the first beast before him, and causeth the earth and them which dwell therein to worship the first beast, whose deadly wound was healed. (Rev. 13:1, 11–12)

The questions and answers on this page and my following page were taken from a Freemasonry training book, which contains 1001 questions and answers. It is where the phrase "a thousand points of light" originated. I am only illustrating questions 22, 24, and 25, which deal with the meaning of five-pointed star and the importance of the sun and moon in Masonry.

Number Twelve   *General Test*

17. What is the derivation of the word symbol?...............................
....
18. What is the meaning of the word emblem?................................
....
19. Of what was the serpent with its tail in its mouth a symbol?
....
20. What is the approximate date of the earliest known hieroglyphics? ....
21. Has the ceremony of baptism any part in Masonry?.................
....
22. Why do the great lights of nature, the sun, moon and Mercury, play an important part in Masonry?..........................
23. What was the name of the Roman soldier who pierced the crucified Saviour with a spear?..
24. What is the symbolism of the five-pointed or "blazing" star?
....
25. In what respect does it symbolize the human body?.................
....

    The answer to question 22 confirms that the sun and the moon, both emblems of Islam, are called along with Mercury, the great lights of Masonry. The answer to question 24 confirms that Masonry inverted Eastern Star represents Lucifer. The answer to question 25 confirms that the five-pointed star, such as those on Rhode Island and other flags, represents a human body. It is like the stars of Hollywood.

Test Number Thirteen   *List of Answers*

live coal. Testing him, the child clapped the burning coal into his mouth, so that he was forever after "slow of speech."
15. The Tau cross.
16. In the form of the cube or double cube. The House of God which King Solomon built was a double cube. The Holy Place was a perfect cube.
17. From sumbulum—that which represents, or a sign of something expressing to the initiate, a doctrine, thought or principle.
18. It is derived from emblema, and first signified work, inlaid-Mosaic work. It now means the same as symbol.
19. Eternity.
20. About 5,000 B.C.
21. It is used in the English rite today.
22. Because every Lodge is a representation of the universe. In our Lodges they constitute the three lights, except that for Mercury the Master of the Lodge has been substituted.
23. Longinus. Tradition says the spear came into the possession of Joseph of Arimathea.
24. It is the Anubis of the Egyptians, giving warning of the overflow of the Nile. It also represents two principles. One point upward, it represents God, good, order, or the Lamb of Ormuzd and St. John. One point downward, it denotes Lucifer, evil, disorder, or the accursed Goat of Mendes.
25. The five points represent the four limbs and head. It is called the sign of the microcosm. All the mysteries of magic were said to be summed up in this symbol.

GENERAL TEST NUMBER THIRTEEN

1. Jerusalem.
2. The Scotch term for Masonic initiation.

Masonry refers to the five-pointed inverted eastern star as the Anubis of the Egyptians. Anubis is the chief god of the underworld among Egyptians and the Greeks. In all sixteen verses of the 31st chapter of Ezekiel, God uses these to describe the Egyptian god of the underworld as Pharaoh. Pharaoh is described as Satan whom God created and made him beautiful. It is a mystery hidden in both the Bible and also within Masonry and their eastern star appendage.

> And it came to pass in the eleventh year, in the third month, in the first day of the month, that the word of the LORD came unto me, saying, Son of man, speak unto Pharaoh king of Egypt, and to his multitude; Whom art thou like in thy greatness?

> Behold, the Assyrian was a cedar in Lebanon with fair branches, and with a shadowing shroud, and of an high stature; and his top was among the thick boughs.

The waters made him great, the deep set him up on high with her rivers running round about his plants, and sent her little rivers unto all the trees of the field.

Therefore his height was exalted above all the trees of the field, and his boughs were multiplied, and his branches became long because of the multitude of waters, when he shot forth. (Ezek. 31:1–5)

The ten remaining verses, beginning with verse 6, confirm Pharaoh as being Satan. This is the reason God hid these stones at the entry to Pharaoh's house and promised to establish the king of Babylon throne upon them and gave him power over all nations, people, and tongues. These are the same stones that Satan challenged Jesus to turn to bread if he be the Son of God. (Matthew 4:1–4)

All the fowls of heaven made their nests in his boughs, and under his branches did all the beasts of the field bring forth their young, and under his shadow dwelt all great nations.

[Note: this includes the G7 leading industrialized nations.]

Thus was he fair in his greatness, in the length of his branches: for his root was by great waters.

The cedars in the garden of God could not hide him: the fir trees were not like his boughs, and the chestnut trees were not like his branches; nor any tree in the garden of God was like unto him in his beauty.

I have made him fair by the multitude of his branches: so that all the trees of Eden, that were in the garden of God, envied him. (Ezek. 31:6–9)

God bought the prophet Ezekiel into His temple and showed him how His people once inside turn their backs to him and worship the sun in the east.

And he brought me into the inner court of the LORD's house, and, behold, at the door of the temple of the LORD, between the porch and the altar, were about five and twenty men, with their backs toward the temple of the LORD, and their faces toward the east; and they worshipped the sun toward the east. (Ezek. 8:16)

But ye have borne the tabernacle of your Moloch and Chiun your images, the star of your god, which ye made to yourselves. (Amos 5:26)

WITCHCRAFT

Woodcut by Francesco Guazzo from *Compendium Maleficarum*, The Newberry Library, Chicago

WORLD BOOK illustration

The Devil Holds Court at the initiation of several witches, *left*, in this artist's portrayal of a witch's rejection of God and dedication to Satan. The star with a goat's face, above, a symbol used in witchcraft, represents Satan.

World Book publishers confirm Freemasonry teaching with the graphics of Satan's inverted star shown on this page. It is the same inverted star on my opposite page taken from the *Eastern Star Book of Adoptive Rite Rituals*. The star inside the apple, which God gave unto me, is positioned upside right in all apples when they are sliced crosswise.

The Lord knew this deception of the Eastern Star would come into the church. Therefore, Paul gave the Church at Corinth a lesson in science, saying,

> There are also celestial bodies, and bodies terrestrial: but the glory of the celestial is one, and the glory of the terrestrial is another.
>
> There is one glory of the sun, and another glory of the moon, and another glory of the stars: for one star differeth from another star in glory. (1 Cor. 15:40–41)

On the eastern star emblem are cunning words imitated from the book of Matthew 2:2, saying, "We have seen his star in the east, and have come to worship him." However, there is nothing in their writing that mention Jesus or he that is born King of the Jews. Rather, the word *fatal* is written on the star to signal *death* to any member who refuses to worship Satan. One of the five icons on the eastern star is the rising sun. One must look closely in order to discern it. This is what they worship. That time has now come.

The forewords of this book of instructions show that the worship of the eastern star was instituted by an act of the United States Congress in 1868. The international headquarters for the Eastern Star is located in Washington, D.C.

Courteously yours,
Robt. Macoy

ADOPTIVE RITE RITUAL

A BOOK OF INSTRUCTION

IN THE

Organization, Government and Ceremonies

OF

CHAPTERS

OF THE ORDER OF THE

EASTERN STAR

ARRANGED BY

ROBERT MACOY

PAST GRAND SECRETARY OF THE SUPREME GRAND CHAPTER

REVISED EDITION

NEW YORK
MACOY PUBLISHING AND MASONIC SUPPLY Co.,
1947

Entered, according to Act of Congress, in the year 1868,
BY THE MASONIC PUBLISHING AND MANUFACTURING COMPANY,
In the Clerk's Office of the District Court of the United States
for the Southern District of New York.

Copyrighted by J. G. BARKER, 1897.
Copyrighted 1928, by
MACOY PUBLISHING AND MASONIC SUPPLY Co.

PREFACE.

HAVING been engaged for a number of years in the dissemination of the beautiful Order of the Eastern Star, and believing that the system is fast becoming deeply rooted in the affections of the Craft and their female relatives; and that the time is not far distant when this system of the Adoptive Rite will receive official recognition, and meet with general acceptance, even where it is now neglected or proscribed, has been the impelling influence for offering this volume upon the plan here suggested.

The want of some systematic organization has been the leading cause in retarding its general usefulness. It may be set down as an axiom, that no degree, however remotely connected with any institution, can take a high place among us unless it possess a well-conceived and philosophic basis of ceremonial, symbolism and constitutional regulation. Without these it is subject to cor-

---

The opening and closing of each Eastern Star chapter is conducted with the special hymns on this and my following page. These hymns cannot be found in traditional Christian hymn books. They are only found in the *Eastern Star Book of Adoptive Rite Rituals and Instructions* to praise and worship the sun.

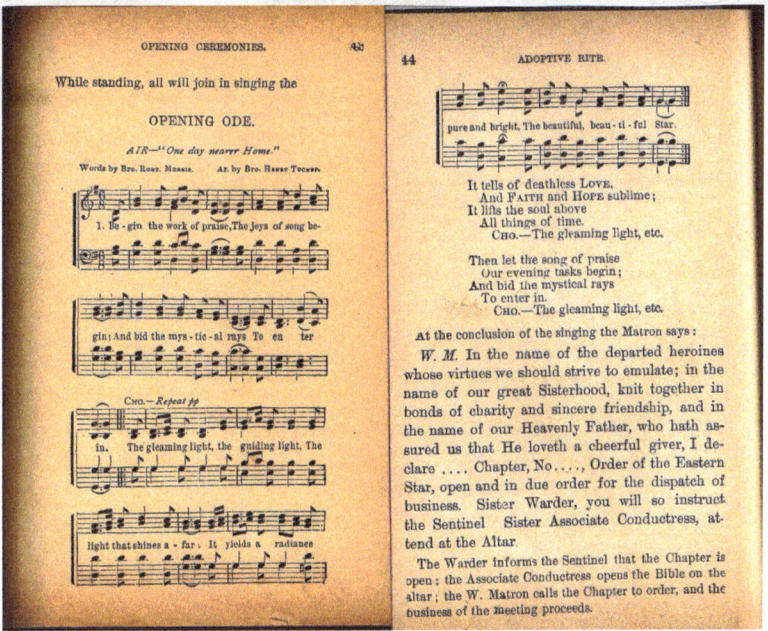

The moon and the sun are the chief emblems of Islam. The emblems of Islam are the crescent moon and a five-pointed star. The star represents the sun, and it is always positioned east of the moon. It is the same crescent and star, which appear as the emblems of Freemasonry Shriners. The Shriners official name is "Ancient Arabic Order of Nobles of the Mystic Shrine." The organization was founded in Mecca, Arabia, in about 644 AD. In 2010, the Shriners changed their name to Shriners International in response to my Revelation. This was my opening message in the proposed Key of David Project Legislation.

While alluding to the sun, which rises in the east and sinks in the west, all Eastern Star members must sing such in their closing hymn of praise.

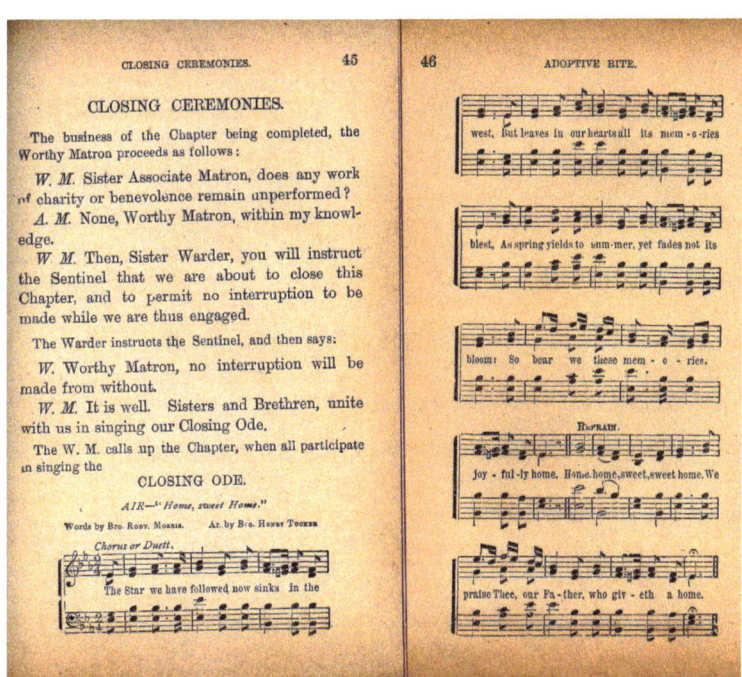

The Eastern Star emblem has on it the image of two beasts. One is a lion, and the other is a young bull calf positioned beside a cross. The star is inverted to deliver by symbolism that this is the Antichrist. The star has fatal written on it to allude to the words of Revelation 13:15, saying, "And he had power to give life unto the image of the beast, that the image of the beast should both speak, and cause that as many as would not worship the image of the beast should be killed."

This threat is enforced supernaturally and can only be neutralized by the power and authority of Jesus Christ. That power dwells with all who put their faith and trust in him as Lord of Lords and King of Kings.

The unveiling and the revelation of America's keystone and its five-pointed pentagram emblem means that God has exposed America's darkest secrets by this stone. This revelation has inspired what The Pentagon has code named "Operation Jade Helm." Jade is a code name for stone, which comes in green and white. The white alludes to Revelation 3:17 whereby Jesus promised to give this white stone called the hidden manna to he who overcomes. It is the promise that inspired the theme song for African American struggles for freedom, justice, and equality.

The color green on the Jade signals the color of most African flags such as Kenya. It signals that God has given this stone to Judah to whom it was promised. With this stone and the star comes power over the nations.

The Five-Sided Pentagon Building, *above;* is the largest office building in the world. It stands across the Potomac River from Washington, D.C.

> And he that overcometh, and keepeth my works unto the end, to him will I give power over the nations: And he shall rule them with a rod of iron; as the vessels of a potter shall they be broken to shivers: even as I received of my Father. And I will give him the morning star. (Rev. 2:26–28)

There are two morning stars. One must remember the apostle Paul's message to the church at Corinth whereby he warned that one star differs from the other in glory. It is this power over the nations given by God to this messenger that has inspired what The Pentagon has code named Operation Jade Helm. The name Helm is synonymous with the Hebrew term *Gilgal*. Gilgal means circle of stones. It was at Gilgal where these twelve stones were laid in the Jordon and the Israelites crossed into Canaan (Josh. 4:1–24).

These twelve stones are symbolized as the foundation of America by placing them as an eleven-point star in the foundation of Liberty. The eleven-point star is used rather than a twelve-point star in order to follow the protocol and the rules of cryptography. In order to encrypt, one must add one or subtract one. The architect for Liberty subtracted one of the points to make it eleven.

STATUE OF LIBERTY

The Statue of Liberty, a symbol of American democracy and a beacon of refuge for immigrants, stands on Liberty Island in New York Harbor. France gave the Statue of Liberty to the United States in 1884 as a gesture of friendship. The monument rises above Fort Wood, built in the shape of an 11-point star during the early 1800's.

33rd Degree Mason

The reason for the biblical description of the men who announced the birth of Jesus as "wise men" has been reserved for God's messenger. These are those who told King Herod that they had seen his star in the east. Why were they called wise men? The answer is the reason the king sought to kill the wise men and the infant Jesus. It is also the reason that the word *fatal* appears on the Eastern Star. The reason is found in Genesis 3:6.

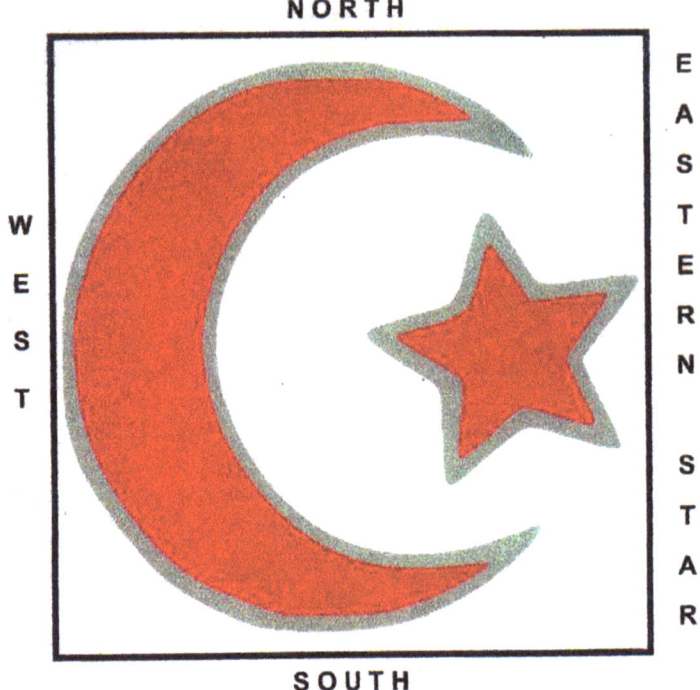

> And when the woman saw that the tree was good for food, and that it was pleasant to the eyes, and a tree to be desired to make one wise, she took of the fruit thereof, and did eat, and gave also unto her husband with her; and he did eat. (Gen. 3:6)

The men had eaten of the fruit where God had hidden this five-pointed star, which is an emblem that contains the knowledge of the Lord Jesus and of Satan. In other words, this star that is found in all apples by slicing them crosswise is an emblem used for both good and evil. This is the definition that is also given by the Freemasons in their training book.

> And the Lord God commanded the man, saying, Of every tree of the garden thou mayest freely eat:
>
> But of the tree of the knowledge of good and evil, thou shalt not eat of it: for in the day that thou eatest thereof thou shalt surely die. (Gen. 2:16–17)

This promised death is the reason that the word *fatal* appears on the Eastern Star. This death is what the Freemasons call the overflow of the Nile. The overflow of the Nile is a metaphoric expression that is used to describe the flood of soldiers, which King Herod dispatched to search, find, and kill the infant Jesus after his identity was confirmed by this secret knowledge of the five-point star.

Verse 6 states that his tree was pleasant to the eyes and to make one wise. It is this truth that inspired what has become known as the Apple iPhone and Apple iPad. It is a divine mystery alluded to by the apostle Paul in 1 Corinthians 1:18–31, when he spoke of God's wisdom.

Chapter 21

Evaluation of Thesis:
Minnesota Graduate School of Theology at
South Texas Bible Institute

It is recorded in my endnotes in chapter 2 that the Lord spoke to me on May 17, 1999, at 2:00 p.m., saying, "This white stone will become a sectional Bible." Therefore, the purpose of this final chapter is to illustrate how the entire 10th chapter of the book of Revelation is devoted to describing this master's degree thesis paper as the little unpublished book that was sealed up. The grade and the actual signed evaluation form of the thesis from Minnesota Graduate School of Theology are also included in this section. There is no other human anywhere in the earth who could have known the secret things published in this paper and articulated them to flow perfectly in each of these twenty-one chapters. If such was possible, then it would have made possible for an imposter to successfully present himself to the world as God's messenger, and the nations and all people would have been deceived. Thus, the kingdom of God would fail and could not come.

Every word of this master's degree thesis was written by me, and it was submitted by a special and unlikely person whom God had chosen and anointed from birth for such a task. It was not known to me neither was it known unto the graduate student. God ordained it to be done covertly so that those who opposed the testimony of God's messenger would also unwittingly confirm and validate it. The grading professor and his staff knew that the words of the thesis were of such a deep and original spiritual nature, that it was impossible for it to have been the words of the submitting student.

The professor deducted ten points because he considered the analysis and deep research was the work of God's messenger rather than the submitting student. He also deducted an additional ten points because having taught the student for several years and had become familiar with her writing style, he knew that this writing style was God's messenger. Man cannot set a limit on the number of words God is allowed for His messenger's testimony. The professor imposed a nineteen thousand word and seventy to seventy-five page limits. The subject could not have been adequately covered had the student adhered to such limitations. Ten additional points were deducted for exceeding the word limit. The paper contains some 39,892 words and a total of 144 pages including the cover, introduction, and table of contents. An additional five points were deducted for something that is not fully clear since the thesis was double-spaced. There were a total of thirty-five superficial points deducted, and no points were deducted because the student failed to reach the objective of the work and prove their points. When these thirty-five points are added back as they were in heaven, the testimony would receive a score of 100 percent. This is because this is an inspired work coming from the Holy Spirit who is perfect in all His ways.

The professor tried to no avail to persuade the student to select another subject to write about rather than the Key of David Project before the US Congress. His efforts continued even until the final days when it was no longer feasible for the student to change subjects. The instructor even cautioned the student that he would not send her paper to Minnesota if she insisted on writing on this Key of David Project that was submitted to Congress by God's messenger. The student was driven by the Spirit of God, and she was unwavering in her determination to fulfill the will of God.

The professor was so prejudice toward the subject that he chose to leave the section for the title blank on the evaluation form. In the end, the professor did the very thing that he sought not to do and the very thing that God had willed him to do. That is to confirm and validate the legitimacy of the Key of David Project proposed legislation and the arrival of Gods' messenger and his testimony unto the nations.

This thesis paper, which has now become a book, is that same little unpublished book that is described in all 11 verses of Revelation chapter 10. It is the book that had sealed up within it, those things that the seven thunders uttered. These have now been unsealed by the Lord Jesus.

STBI SOUTH TEXAS BIBLE INSTITUTE / Minnesota Graduate School of Theology

Thesis – Dissertation Evaluation Form

___PATRICIA FRANKLIN_____ _____
   Name of Student   Subject Title

Evaluation of Thesis: (Superior, Excellent, Great, Good, (Fair,) Poor)

1. **Contents of Paper:** ___EXCEEDED THE WORD LIMIT -10___
   [Did the student meet the 19k word requirement for MA (approx 70-75 pages) / 45k word requirement for ThD (approx 170-180 pages) / 50k word requirement for PhD (approx 180-190 pages), if not, **deduct 10 points**]

2. **Analysis (Depth of Research):** ___YES (BUT NOT HER WORK) -10___
   [Did the student have sufficient # of footnotes – anything less than 10 footnotes for MA, or 30 footnotes for ThD/PhD- **deduct 15 points**]

3. **Adherence to Specified Subject:** ___YES___
   [Is there a thesis statement in the introduction…if not deduct **5 points**]

4. **Writing Style:** ___NOT HER OWN WORDS   -10___
   ✓ [Does the student's train of thought flow properly…if not **deduct points objectively**]
   ___[Does the student reach the objective of the work (prove their point)…if not **deduct points objectively**]

5. **Footnotes, Spelling, Typing, Etc.:** _____
   ___[Footnotes should be at the end of each page, or at the end of each chapter…if not done correctly, **deduct 5 points**]
   ___[Did the student follow the guidelines for the cover page….if not, **deduct 15 points**]
   ✓ [Did the student double space…if not **deduct 5 points**] BOTH SIDES -5
   ___[Did the student leave 1 inch margins on all sides…if not **deduct 5 points**]
   ___[Did the student leave more than 1 inch space between Chapters or paragraphs…if so, deduct 5 points]
   ___[Did the student place their Table of Contents on the next page following the Cover page…if not, **deduct 5 points**]
   ___[Did the student type their work in Times New Roman – 12 font…if not, **deduct 10 points**]
   ___[Did the student turn in their project with the proper binding (spiral bind with clear plastic cover for MA, professionally bound with designed cover for ThD/PhD…if not, **deduct 10 points**]
   ___[Did the student provide 3 copies of their final work…if not, deduct 5 points]

Other Comments: ___TIME AND EFFORT WERE HERS. TOO MUCH COPYING OF OTHERS WORK AND NOT ENOUGH OF HER OWN WORDS.___ (65) D

Thesis/ Dissertation Grade: ___D___

Reviewed By: ___Dr. ___ ThD___

Date: ___5-2-2015___

A	100 – 90%	Excellent
B	89 – 80%	Good
C	79 – 70%	Average
(D)	69 – 60%	Poor
F	59 or below	Failure
I	incomplete	Incomplete

The twelve memorial stones of the exodus representing the twelve tribes of Israel became the Great Seal of the United States. These are numbered from A-1 to L-12 on the US one-dollar bill with an Egyptian pyramid, which symbolizes their origin. These have been assembled together and raised as a pillar, which has become known as the Washington Monument. Its height of 555 feet was calculated according to the height of seven pillars measured according to Cleopatra's Needle in New York Central Park. These pillars were raised to the sun goddess Isis, and they are called pillars of fire in Revelation chapter 10:1. These pillars became the symbolic feet of the angel whose face shine as the sun to send an encrypted biblical message about this great mystery. The stones that are called pillars of fire inspired the name of what is called "firestone tires." A tire is circular to symbolize Gilgal where these stones were laid in the Jordan (Josh. 4:1–24). Gilgal is a Hebrew word that means circle of stones. The phrase "Jade Helm" migrated from this word because Jade is a stone and Helm is the wheel. Therefore, chapter 10 of the book of Revelation begins with these words:

> And I saw another mighty angel come down from heaven, clothed with a cloud: and a rainbow was upon his head, and his face was as it were the sun, and his feet as pillars of fire: And he had in his hand a little book open: and he set his right foot upon the sea, and his left foot on the earth. (Rev. 10:1–2)

This riddle alludes to his right foot standing upon these where the Statue of Liberty is positioned in the harbor with these seven pillars of fire as her crown and rays of sun. His left foot is on the earth where the Washington Monument stands as eight pillars joined as one. The little book is the substance of this master's degree thesis, which was all sealed until now.

> And cried with a loud voice, as when a lion roareth: and when he had cried, seven thunders uttered their voices.
>
> And when the seven thunders had uttered their voices, I was about to write: and I heard a voice from heaven saying unto me, Seal up those things which the seven thunders uttered, and write them not. (Rev. 10:3–4)

The seven thunders are the substance of the seven seals, which contain those things that have never been uttered or written. For the angel said, "Seal them up, and write them not." The Lord Jesus commanded that I keep a systematic diary of the things that were uttered to me by the Holy Spirit so that it bare witness for the origin of my testimony. These began in April 1998, and they have continued systematically until the date of this thesis.

> And the angel which I saw stand upon the sea and upon the earth lifted up his hand to heaven,
>
> And sware by him that liveth for ever and ever, who created heaven, and the things that therein are, and the earth, and the things that therein are, and the sea, and the things which are therein, that there should be time no longer:
>
> But in the days of the voice of the seventh angel, when he shall begin to sound, the mystery of God should be finished, as he hath declared to his servants the prophets. (Rev. 10:5–7)

Since the sound of the voice of the seventh angel signals a turning point and that time should be no more, then I must illustrate when and what causes the voice of the seventh angel to sound. The seventh angel sounds only after God's messenger is killed by the beast and is raised up from the dead by God before all nations. He then ascends up to heaven in a cloud. As a witness for God, among other things, we are to testify and prove that God is able to raise the dead. This mystery is in the 11th chapter of Revelation, which is purposely followed by and is essentially a continuation of chapter 10. I will illustrate this from chapter 11 so that I may continue the flow of clarity for this mystery, and then after doing so, I will return to chapter 10.

Operation Jade Helm 15 is an escalation of the war where the beast will kill God's messenger. I will begin with the portion of chapter 11 to show when the voice of the seventh angel will sound.

> And when they shall have finished their testimony, the beast that ascendeth out of the bottomless pit shall make war against them, and shall overcome them, and kill them.
>
> And their dead bodies shall lie in the street of the great city, which spiritually is called Sodom and Egypt, where also our Lord was crucified.
>
> And they of the people and kindreds and tongues and nations shall see their dead bodies three days and an half, and shall not suffer their dead bodies to be put in graves.
>
> And they that dwell upon the earth shall rejoice over them, and make merry, and shall send gifts one to another; because these two prophets tormented them that dwelt on the earth.
>
> And after three days and an half the spirit of life from God entered into them, and they stood upon their feet; and great fear fell upon them which saw them.
>
> And they heard a great voice from heaven saying unto them, Come up hither. And they ascended up to heaven in a cloud; and their enemies beheld them.
>
> And the same hour was there a great earthquake, and the tenth part of the city fell, and in the earthquake were slain of men seven thousand: and the remnant were affrighted, and gave glory to the God of heaven.
>
> The second woe is past; and, behold, the third woe cometh quickly [the seventh angel and the seventh trumpet sounds].
>
> And the seventh angel sounded; and there were great voices in heaven, saying, The kingdoms of this world are become the kingdoms of our Lord, and of his Christ; and he shall reign for ever and ever.
>
> And the nations were angry, and thy wrath is come, and the time of the dead, that they should be judged, and that thou shouldest give reward unto thy servants the prophets, and to the saints, and them that fear thy name, small and great; and shouldest destroy them which destroy the earth.
>
> And the temple of God was opened in heaven, and there was seen in his temple the ark of his testament: and there were lightnings, and voices, and thunderings, and an earthquake, and great hail. (Rev. 11:7–19)

These foregoing has clearly shown what triggers the sound of the seventh angel. It is the war with the beast joined by the nations against God and His messenger. The phrase "trumpet sound" is used as a deep metaphor under several veils to represent war. It is war against the army of God, which has already come down from heaven into the earth and its atmosphere. Before returning to the 10th chapter of Revelation, I shall go to the 16th chapter of Revelation to show that the sound of the seventh angel ushers in what is called in the Hebrew tongue Armageddon.

As God's two witnesses, we testify and prove that God raised Jesus from the dead and that he likewise would raise us before all kindred, nations, and tongues. We are two in one. The photo on this and my next page shows both the man and angelic forms of God's two witnesses. We are the same two in one who witnessed the resurrection of Jesus, which is coded in the four gospels as two in one. And we are the same two witnesses who witnessed his ascension in Acts 1:10–11. This two-in-one gift is reserved for all believers who shall be changed into their immortal bodies in the twinkle of an eye. This shall happen with the sound of the last trump. It is a mystery.

Behold, I shew you a mystery; We shall not all sleep, but we shall all be changed, In a moment, in the twinkling of an eye, at the last trump: for the trumpet shall sound, and the dead shall be raised incorruptible, and we shall be changed. For this corruptible must put on incorruption, and this mortal must put on immortality. (1 Cor. 15:51–53)

It would be a dreadful and regrettable mistake to assume that Operation Jade Helm 15 is limited to the United States' military. It shall also be a mistake to assume that by remaining silent, you are aiding God rather than Satan. Jesus spoke of this day in Matthew 12:30 when he said, "He that is not with me is against me; and he that gathereth not with me scattereth abroad." All the kings of the earth shall line up with the beast to fight against God and His army, which has come down from heaven.

> And I saw three unclean spirits like frogs come out of the mouth of the dragon, and out of the mouth of the beast, and out of the mouth of the false prophet. For they are the spirits of devils, working miracles, which go forth unto the kings of the earth and of the whole world, to gather them to the battle of that great day of God Almighty.

> Behold, I come as a thief. Blessed is he that watcheth, and keepeth his garments, lest he walk naked, and they see his shame.

> And he gathered them together into a place called in the Hebrew tongue Armageddon. And the seventh angel poured out his vial into the air; and there came a great voice out of the temple of heaven, from the throne, saying, It is done.

> And there were voices, and thunders, and lightnings; and there was a great earthquake, such as was not since men were upon the earth, so mighty an earthquake, and so great.
>
> And the great city was divided into three parts, and the cities of the nations fell: and great Babylon came in remembrance before God, to give unto her the cup of the wine of the fierceness of his wrath.
>
> And every island fled away, and the mountains were not found. And there fell upon men a great hail out of heaven, every stone about the weight of a talent: and men blasphemed God because of the plague of the hail; for the plague thereof was exceeding great. (Rev. 16:13–21)

> An Actual Angelic Photo of the Prophet Elijah

> Behold, I will send you Elijah the prophet before the coming of the great and dreadful day of the LORD:
>
> And he shall turn the heart of the fathers to the children, and the heart of the children to their fathers, lest I come and smite the earth with a curse. (Mal. 4:5–6)

It must be noted that the nations and all its leaders have a secret plan to keep Satan and his kingdoms in place. A worldwide campaign has long begun to portray Satan as a good man. He is not a man. He is an evil and adverse spirit whose aim is to pull those who worship him into the pit where he is destined. This thesis may be used for preparing yourselves both spiritually and physically for the most challenging times in the history of mankind.

There shall be critical water shortages that may surpass those of California and Nevada. Digging wells in the deserts will serve little or no purpose. Your water must flow from the fountain created when the Lord was pierced and wounded for our transgressions. No need to join the National Rifle Association and take up arms against the Lord and his anointed. He that seeks to live by the sword shall also die by the sword. The Lord has been given the keys to both death and hell. Those who seek death for others or themselves must go through him who is holding these keys.

> And in those days shall men seek death, and shall not find it; and shall desire to die, and death shall flee from them. (Rev. 9:6)
>
> I am he that liveth, and was dead; and, behold, I am alive for evermore, Amen; and have the keys of hell and of death. (Rev. 1:18)

In preparation for dealing with the water shortages that shall bring on food shortages, NASA has sent up two identical spacecraft that are appropriately named GRACE (Gravity Recovery and Climate Experiment). They are flying about 220 kilometers apart in a polar orbit, 500 kilometers above the earth mapping for water. As part of the war to win souls to Christ and usher in the kingdom of God, God has given us power over waters.

> And I will give power unto my two witnesses, and they shall prophesy a thousand two hundred and threescore days, clothed in sackcloth.
>
> These have power to shut heaven, that it rain not in the days of their prophecy: and have power over waters to turn them to blood, and to smite the earth with all plagues, as often as they will. (Rev. 11:3, 6)

All these plagues may be placed in abeyance once those things, outlined in the Key of David Project, are implemented. God takes no pleasure in bringing hardship to those for whom he gave his life. To do so would be counterproductive.

> He shall forever be called

the God of salvation,

and he has never been known as the God of damnation.

Accept Him today

without cost.

Ellis island and its mysteries are God's gift to Prophet Ellis.

Her lamp sheds light on a golden door.